The Road Unseen:
A Paranormal Journey Into High Strangeness

By

Dennis W Carroll and Brandon Hudgens

Paralina Publishing

Cover photo by Dennis W Carroll
Cover design by Brandon Hudgens and Dennis W. Carroll
Book design by Brandon Hudgens and Dennis W. Carroll

ISBN: 978-0-9898020-6-2
First Printing: December, 2014

Life is infinitely stranger than anything which the mind of man could invent.

Arthur Conan Doyle

It is thought by many experts that 75 to 80% of the known universe is invisible and remains unseen.

Anonymous

The authors wish to state that the following subject matters are in part based on supposition and conjecture and are not necessarily the only explanations for the mysteries we have committed ourselves to examine. The sole purpose of this book is to expose the reader to the subjects. Our hope is that you will continue to search for the true answers and travel down the road unseen.

The Road Unseen

Beyond the shadows of this life,
Beyond the blue and the green.
The shade of another world is waiting,
Down, a road unseen.

This unknown land is always with us,
Just at the edge of our sight.
Some have the courage to go there,
Fearing not, to leave the light.

Far past the boundaries of life and death,
Of what is real and what is dream.
The answers lie waiting before us,
Somewhere down, this road unseen.

So let us go once more my friend,
to where the mysteries may gleam,
Beyond the known, into tomorrow,
Down... the road unseen.

Dennis W. Carroll

High Strangeness

In the realm of the supernatural and the paranormal things that are weird occasionally become even weirder. There are things in this world that are far above and beyond what is even considered normal for the supernatural and the paranormal, then we begin to see and encounter High Strangeness.

So, the authors have defined High Strangeness as the situations and experiences that can sometimes take you far beyond all human understanding.

There seem to be elements in this world that have no rhyme or reason in the execution of their actions. They hide always behind a veil of the unknown and play their little games with us, all the while laughing at our bafflement with sly grins as they twist us first one way, then another, feeding off our doubts and fears. Always knowing how near impossible it is for us to pin them down. All of these things are but wearers of masks, they are not really what they may appear to be, but it is the thing behind the mask that we, as paranormal researchers, are concerned with chiefly.

Preface

For many years there have been rumors, and perhaps even clues, to a shadow world beyond our own. This shadow presence is ever lurking behind almost every facet of our society and even our very civilization itself. Those involved deeply in the study of the supernatural and the paranormal have from time to time caught brief glimpses of this very secretive initiative. For some, this knowledge has come with a high price and perhaps in some cases, even a deadly one. This force hidden in the shadows is as old as the stars themselves and it guards well the secrets of its nature and operations. It might well be that as the authors of what you are about to read, we could be putting our very lives and well being at risk, but we feel that it is time for us and for you to travel, the road unseen.

Chapter One

Passing Strange

Life is either a daring adventure or nothing at all.

Helen Keller

Dennis' Story

I have always been fascinated with the area of paranormal research dealing with UFO's. I never dreamed that one day I too would have my own encounter and rub shoulders with high strangeness. In my forty plus years of studying research and investigation in the many fields of the paranormal, I have seen many strange things. You can get to a point sometimes when you think you've seen it all and I have felt that way a little…how very wrong I was.

My UFO encounter began for me one fall day in the year 2008. At that time I was walking for exercise on a regular basis. I love to walk and still do with my dog Zach (a very curious and sensitive black and white cocker spaniel). Together he and I log at least a mile or two whenever possible. I feel that walking is one of the most enjoyable forms of exercise that there is, but the time I am writing about was before I had Zach.

For a long time I had walked at a local mall, especially during the hot and humid summers we have. This particular instance I had gotten bored with the mall and since the fall weather had begun I moved my walking outside. I'm a big lover of the outdoors. I had started walking downtown on a circuit of blocks that I followed to achieve a distance of a few miles. My hometown of Anderson, South Carolina is what I would now term as a small to midsize town but still continues to a grow at a healthy pace. Like a few of the surrounding mid-sized southern towns, it still manages to hang on to a little of its old southern small town feeling.

Unfortunately that is rapidly becoming a thing of the past. I had parked at the south end of town, across the road from the city hall and police station, next to a closed down diner that had once been and still is, a landmark in the city. It had sadly seen its best days in the late sixties. It also stands next to a news stand and bookstore that held many fond memories for me, as it was a hangout for me in my younger years when I went there as a kid many times to buy comic books and horror magazines (famous Monsters of Film-land was my favorite). Anyway, the time of day was almost twilight. I had just finished my walk and was cooling down before I started to head to my car that was parked nearby. Now, at the left side of this empty diner there is nothing but space, a vacant lot that steeply declines to the level lot below and behind the buildings in this part of town. A chain link fence borders this drop off at the sidewalk. Downtown Anderson shuts down pretty much around six o'clock every evening, although further down there a few places that remain open longer like the restaurants and such. However, at this time there was very little traffic and noise that accompanies it. There was, also, no foot traffic in the slightly run down section where I was walking. Keep that point in mind. Well, I was standing there on the sidewalk with a hand on the fence, at the corner of this building and empty lot, looking up and out beyond the level below toward the sun that had just mostly set. Something on the distant horizon immediately caught my eye. I had first seen it at the edge of my vision and then looked at it head on.

During my lifetime I have been interested in many fields of study, criminology, biology, and what I call my four A's (Anthropology, Astronomy, Archeology, and Aeronautics), among others. I am familiar with everything that mankind has made to fly, but what I saw in the sky that evening was unlike anything I had ever seen before or since. The autumn sky was overcast and clouds were hanging quite low that day and a few street lights had already come on. Having an interest in weather, I know that low hanging clouds can mean rain, so I had been keeping an eye on the clouds, especially during my walk. As I said before, it was almost twilight and there was a slight autumn mist in the air as well. What I saw, or rather the shape that I could make out was huge and triangular. However, the object itself was hidden by the low hanging clouds as it steadily and quickly made its way to my position. I could however see its silhouette. It never stopped or slowed in its flight. There was, however, a part of the craft and I have to say that is what it was, a craft, there was a part that resembled a platform of some sort that was observable below the clouds, at the bottom of the object. The part I could see was black like the shape of the thing itself and it had a very weird and very slight purplish glow to it. It moved very swiftly right over my head and I turned to watch it as it did so. It disappeared unnaturally fast over town and a nearby church steeple and I lost it, in what the little of the horizon that I could see. All the while it had been completely and absolutely, eerily silent. There were no traffic sounds at all to mask it. This thing was really huge and was absolutely quiet and silent in its run over my head. It had no markings or running lights of any kind. I was astounded to say the least. I was not thinking at all of anything like that happening. The subject of UFOs, at that moment, was far from any thought in my mind. It was no balloon, it was no blimp, it was no glider and everything that I had ever seen up until then that could fly like that, makes some kind of a noise. Other than what little I could see of it, the eerie silence of this thing raised the hairs on the back of my neck. It was other worldly but also in a strange way had a militaristic look to it as well. The question remained was who or what's military?

That night, after I told a few people of my experience over the phone (a few days later, I even emailed my sighting to MUFON, but never heard anything back), I thought that all this was the end of my brush with high strangeness…how very wrong I was, for this was only just the beginning.

A few days later, things really started getting weird. First, there were the strange phone calls. All that they consisted of were garbled, mechanical sounds inter mingled with howling wind like noises. I got to listen to these on my answering machine quite often. Sometimes I received a couple of calls a day. One time, the machine recorded what sounded like a weird indecipherable radio transmission of some kind. I have never heard of an answering machine picking up on a radio call like that, but I guess it's possible. This happened off and on for a while and then the van showed up. It was a black unmarked government van, the Econoline series type van. The van was completely black, with black tinted windows and a plainly seen government tag. It always buzzed my house at dusk, at least once a week and that was after I started noticing it. Once I noticed the van its visits became a little more unpredictable. I of course became very curious and I hate to say it but a little paranoid as well.

I began a systematic search of the surrounding area of where I live, with an ever widening and expanding circular search pattern. I was thinking that maybe someone that worked for the government perhaps lived close by, but there were no results. There were a couple of times too when I suspected someone of prowling around my yard at night, but I could never really pin anything down. I just had a feeling of things not being "right." I was beginning to think that I was living in a John Keel book or the mothman prophecies movie.

The weird feelings these types of happenings give you are unsettling to say the least, especially when you have to hesitate in telling your friends, simply because they probably won't believe you. It is a very lonely thing when you are living in a situation that no one will believe. It is one of the loneliest of experiences you can ever have.

Finally, after a few more weeks of this, the phone calls stopped and the van disappeared, except for that one last time I saw it. It was at twilight, a couple of weeks after I had begun to breathe a little easier, as everything had seemed to have gotten back to normal. I was coming out of K-mart and I spotted it, way out in the parking lot. I knew it immediately when I saw it, without any doubt. I started toward it then, determined to get to the bottom of all this. I was half way to the van in that almost deserted parking lot, when something stopped me dead in my tracks.

I'm the kind of guy, who my whole life, never has backed down from anything. I don't claim to be fearless, but there hasn't ever been much that has spooked me. The strangest feeling came over me just then, that if I got to that van I was going to die or disappear, or both. As I stood there thinking my choices over, the lights of the van came on and it slowly drove away. I do wonder what would have happened to me that day if I hadn't stopped in that parking lot, but I have learned one important lesson from my run in with high strangeness and that is this. When you look into the things of the paranormal, they sometimes will start looking back at you. As in the case of the hunter and the hunted, so it is with high strangeness, it can also sometimes, come looking for you.

Brandon's Story

I must admit that I had never heard the phrase "High Strangeness" until I met Dennis. I forget now how the conversation began, but I remember him saying those two words for the first time. My eyes squinted and my head turned slightly when he said it. Apparently he saw the confounded look on my face, because he then began to explain High Strangeness to me.

I never in my life would have believed that there was another world vastly larger than ghost hunting. It also amazes me how interconnected High Strangeness is with ghost hunting. For instance, some reports have been made by individuals that have witnessed a UFO, of increased ghostly activity. High Strangeness encompasses so much that the only roadblock that I had for research was time.

From the first time that I heard the words "High Strangeness" I knew that I was in for the long haul. I have been a paranormal investigator for some time now and have witnessed many strange events, but High Strangeness probably has become more of an interest to me over the last few years. I think because High Strangeness involves more than just ghosts and spirits. Don't get me wrong, I still love a good ghost investigation but to me there seems to be more and more connections to ghosts, spirits, and High Strangeness.

For years I had no idea that I actually had a High Strangeness encounter when I was younger. I witnessed something that I never could explain, until Dennis had mentioned Elementals to me. The story I want to share I had never told anyone outside of my family until Dennis and I began this book. As we were discussing the varying degrees of High Strangeness I told him of an encounter I had when I was a boy that I never quite worked out in my head. I told him that I saw this small creature that stood no more than two feet tall with sharp teeth and pointed ears. That was the only description I gave to him. Dennis immediately said that I had an encounter with an Elemental.

After our quick discussion, I decided to look into Elementals. I found that these beings come in a variety of packages that correlate to the elements of Earth, Wind, Water, and Fire. I was drawn to the descriptions of the Earth Elementals. Here there were varying beings being described, but one in particular stood out to me. I saw the descriptions of Gnomes.

As I have said, I have never told anyone outside of my family about my encounter because I really had no clue what I was looking at. I was probably around the age of nine or ten at the time. I can't quite remember my age, but I remember the day of the encounter so vividly I can still remember what the air smelled like.

I remember that I was on summer break from school and my mom forced me to go outside quite a bit. I believe it was more for her sanity than it was for me getting fresh air. This particular day was very beautiful. It was not hot, even though we were in the dog days of summer, the sky was a beautiful bright blue with specks of huge white clouds floating steadily through the air, there was the slightest breeze blowing, and I was sitting on a hill on the side of my yard enjoying the magnificence of the day.

My grandmother had a small mutt that we named Bruiser that absolutely loved me and followed me everywhere I went. I enjoyed having him because he was a great at steering me away from snakes. Bruiser was lying at my side enjoying the day as much as I was. I was almost asleep when I heard a rustling noise next to a workshop that my grandfather had just built. When I looked over I saw, what I assumed to be, the biggest field rat I had ever laid eyes on. When looked closer I noticed that this "field rat" was standing on its hind legs. I thought that this was rather strange but I then thought that maybe it was trying find a way into my grandfather's workshop. When I sat up, it saw me. That is when I realized that what I was staring at was no field rat; it was no kind of rat that I had ever laid eyes on.

This creature was bi-pedal. It stood about two feet tall, with what I can only perceive as hands, and its skin was a hairless brownish green. We stared at each other for a few moments. Its face was oval with pointed ears and a sunken nose. It had large obsidian eyes that glistened in the sun. As we stared at each other not moving and me hardly breathing, this thing suddenly let out a snarling hiss.

This hiss captured the attention of Bruiser. He looked up and I could see him stiffen. I knew that he was about to give chase. I didn't want Bruiser to go after this thing, so I grabbed him before he could jump up. About this time the short bi-pedal creature began to run. Being curious, I jumped up and chased it at a safe distance because I didn't want a close encounter with this thing.

As I turned the corner of the workshop, I saw the creature dive into a stack of bricks that were left over from the construction of the workshop. He was trapped, so I did the only thing that a sensible ten-year-old would do, I found a stick and began poking through the openings of the stack of bricks. Bruiser was even running around sniffing at the bricks. I just followed him around and when he gave attention to a certain area, I would poke the stick there.

When I was satisfied that the creature was not going to come after Bruiser or me, I began to remove the bricks one by one. It took me a good half hour to even move half of the bricks. I finally came to spot where I saw a hole in the ground.

I was excited at this point. I just knew that I was going to capture this thing. I ran the stick down the hole until I found the bottom. I was confused at first and then I realized that the hole that I was poking around in was, at one point, a fence post hole.

That is when confusion really set in. How did this creature get away from us? When did it slip out of our sight? What was this thing really? I had a million questions.

I decided that if this creature did go in the hole, I was not going to let it come back out of it. I then loaded the hole completely with small bricks. Once I was satisfied that no more bricks were going into the hole, I began to put larger bricks on top of the opening. I was finally satisfied enough that this creature was going to have to burrow its way out if it wanted out.

I told Bruiser to go home and I then went home. I ran to my grandmother's house, found her, and told her exactly what just happened. I thought that she was going to tell me it was a figment of my imagination, but to my surprise she raised her eyebrows and said, "Really?" She moved to the window to look out toward the bricks and asked me if I were sure that I covered the hole well enough. I told her I thought I did and asked her if she believed me.

She looked at me slightly trembling and said, "Yes. I do actually."

I was shocked. My grandmother was a deeply religious woman that generally dismissed tales of this kind. That is when she told me that she knew someone else that had the exact same encounter, with the exact same creature about fifteen years prior. My jaw dropped. She never would tell me who had the experience, but I did have my suspicions.

At ten years old, I had my first encounter with High Strangeness. It wasn't until recently that I knew exactly what it was I saw. Even now, I am trying to confirm my sighting with the other person. When I mention it to them they quickly change the subject and move far away from it as possible. This tells me that I was not dreaming that warm breezy day. Every time I am at my mom's house now I look down at the spot where that stack of bricks once was and wonder if I will ever get a glimpse of my Gnome again.

Chapter Two

Stranger Than Strange

I cannot tell how the truth may be; I say the tale as it was said to me

Sir Walter Scott

Personal Case File

Dennis Carroll

As paranormal investigators, we have seen and experienced many weird and strange things, first hand. We also hear the paranormal related stories of others and their experiences as well. Just recently, this report was given to us of a former law enforcement officer and his very strange experience. He is now a long haul truck driver and an extremely no nonsense kind of fellow.

One spring, he was in his trailer truck and leaving California on a mountain valley pass highway. It was at night and he had just started his shift, so he says he was fully awake. He came up on another truck which was slower than him. He passed the truck that was not going very fast and as he was checking his mirrors to move back over, this full size 18 wheeler was no longer there. He stated implicitly, that there was not enough time for it to have gotten out of sight, as he was right beside it and there was no other road or turn off it could have taken. It just suddenly wasn't there, anymore.

Where did that very large truck go? Was it the ghost of trucker, who may perhaps have died on that stretch of highway? Was the truck ever really there to start with or was it something that could be seen, but was also not in the same reality with us? Many questions, with very few answers, but we keep searching for the truth. As that is what paranormal research and investigation is all about, a search for the truth.

Another recent incident that we had reported, concerns a Lady friend of ours, who came home one day in the afternoon and found herself facing what can possibly be termed as some kind of strange dimensional shift, of time and space.

Here is her story as she told it to me.

The day I experienced the time/space reality shift we had company outside and I had gone in the house to check on the wash, I was washing clothes. I took the clothes out of the washer and put them in the dryer, then I turned to go back outside and all of a sudden it was as if the hallway was a mile long. It looked as if this hallway in my house had suddenly stretched. I stood looking down the hallway and could see the people outside but it looked as if they were a long way away from me. I could hear their voices but it was as if they were talking in slow motion. My heart was pounding and I was terrified. Everything around me just didn't seem or feel right. It was as if I were out of place. I didn't think I would ever reach the end of the hall but when I did it was like everything was back to normal. I turned back to look down the hall and it was normal looking again. I went on outside to where my guests were, but it was a while before I felt comfortable enough to go back inside. My daughter-in-law also experienced the same thing there once in that house as well.

Over the years we have had reports of many of these time and space dimensional shifts. A lot of these incidents are supported by theories in quantum physics and mechanics. Now let's look a little into some of the meta-physical aspects, in some cases we've had. Here is a report that we received from a very straight forward kind of practical fellow, who just wanted some answers to his encounter with the unknown. Here is his account, unedited.

Hey Guys, sorry I didn't go into detail with the situation. I wasn't sure if the comment box was limited to so many characters or not, so I kept it short just to get the emails going. To my knowledge there has only been one death on the property. There are several houses sitting on the land and the death that I'm aware of is in the barn/apartment to the right of my mobile home. I've been living there for about a year now and I've had some strange things happen that have gradually turned into some things where I truly felt terrified and even threatened.

The first thing I can really remember happening was the sound of a kid that sounded like he was crying or murmuring something. At the time I had a roommate and dismissed it as his T.V. being on or something and the timer cutting off just as I approached his doorway to listen further. I wrote it off as simple timing but I still couldn't help but ask my roommate if he had a movie in his DVD player with a kid crying. There was no such movie with any scene like that so that kept me curious about the situation but I never heard it again. The next thing I had happen was the sound of a pair of heavy boots pacing back and forth in a storage room just outside my bedroom backdoor. I woke to the sound of these boots going back and forth in this small room. As I listened and became a little more aware I was convinced it wasn't the puppies or rabbits under my trailer chasing each other around. These were very deliberate steps and I began to hear the sound of tissue paper tearing in the room. I couldn't help but think this guy in heavy boots was tearing the pages out of a Bible or something like that. I got up and cut the lights on readied my gun just in case someone came through the door. Nothing ever came and the steps ended shortly after I prepared myself for some drunken invasion from a Bible hating homeless man or something. A few months would pass before anything else substantial would occur. The next thing to happen was while I was in the shower. As I turned to face the shower head after rinsing out my hair the shower curtain fluttered like someone ran their hand across the other side to the shower head, then I caught a shadow of a arm against the wall stretching out towards the shower head as I turned. I was startled but once more, I dismissed it as me turning and somehow the shower curtain cast the shadow if maybe I bumped it during my turn. While I am very much a believer in the paranormal and all things involved I've grown to try and write off these happenings as nothing more than simple moments caught in a funny way.

I've had many things happen in my life through my 28 (almost 29) years where I've seen, heard and encountered what I believe to be ghosts or something else. So I'm going to jump into a little side story about one of my assumptions for why this place has something going on. My first experience with an Ouija board produced incredible results for me, my cousin and my nephew. I'll skip the details on everything that happened for now but I will tell you we didn't know what we were doing and we didn't know we were suppose to send it back or tell it goodbye or anything. So I'm the one that has kept the board the entire time since I can't help but wonder if that could be the reasoning so many strange things have been happening. Back to the one death I'm aware of on the property. This old barn was converted into an apartment at one point and a guy there passed away in it in the past couple of years as a result of what was called an overdose. He was up there with two women, they left and they said they came back and found him dead. We have always been curious if they had any part in his OD and left to cover their own tracks and say they found him that way. Maybe it was just as they said. They found him. But it all seemed convenient to me about how he died in the short span they were gone. But I'm not writing you guys to point fingers or play detective. But that is the story of the one death I know of.

Back to the house things went quiet for a couple months once again with only minor sounds happening that I could easily write as animals in the area. I came home one night after work and that day

I didn't get a chance to feed my dog so I was heading out to feed him. It was around 10-11pm I believe and I was coming up to his dog house with the food when I heard a small pitter patter of feet run right up behind me and I could have sworn I felt a short gust of air on the back of my neck when it stopped behind me. I spun around casting my brand new LED flashlights beam behind me. I expected to see the puppies, or a chicken or maybe a rabbit behind me but there was nothing. I looked further down into the woods but there was nothing. I had a very eerie feeling, a very strong feeling then of being watched and I noticed how quiet it was. My dog wasn't barking, the hunting dogs behind me weren't barking, everything was eerily quiet. Every time I go to feed my dog, no matter what time in the day, the hunting dogs always come out and bark and howl, but there was nothing. It was just a looming feeling that something was with me. As I continued to shine my light, I noticed something very strange with the light. Keep in mind this was a brand new flashlight at the time. I was casting my light from left to right panning across the path and as my light would come back to center it would flicker as if there was some kind of interference. The first couple of times I just assumed the batteries were dying or the light was faulty. Then I began to notice it would only flicker in one place in particular which was directly in front of me and where I heard the footsteps.

I took off running back to my house actually freaked out this time. A couple weeks later I gave my dog his flea bath and medicine and decided I was going to keep him inside for a few days while his meds kicked in and maybe see if he could help find something that was taking place in the house. I was beginning to feel like something was now here, after I heard the steps. I felt eyes on me when I would watch tv or would constantly get a feeling of being watched while I slept and I could not stay asleep for long periods. So maybe my dog would help out with things for a couple days and see what happened. The first night he was in the house I was in bed when I woke up once again with the feeling I was being watched. I looked down to the foot of my bed, down the short hallway and into the living room where my couch was, that sat against the front wall facing my bedroom. It was in a direct line of sight to the couch from my bed. And that was when I seen it. I was still half asleep and the light shone just enough to make out what was on my couch. It looked like a person sitting upright, one arm propped up on the arm rest and staring right at me. But the thing was, it seemed to have the face of a dog, same colors and markings as my pit bull. It was smiling at me with this huge exaggerated smile that just seemed to stretch further and further the longer I stared. With it looking just like my dog I couldn't help but call his name out, maybe it was just how he was sitting with some couch pillows and blankets that gave him the shape of a person sitting up and the smile was just from me being half asleep. So when I called his name I was expecting him to jump off the couch and come into my room, but when I said it, he popped up from beside my bed, where he was sound asleep. I was terrified, what was sitting on my couch. I didn't want to look again. I laid my head back down and just forced my eyes closed. I could hear the floor in the living room bending and cracking as it always does when someone walks on it. Then it went quiet and I finally fell asleep.

The very next morning as I came out of the shower, I was singing, and my dog was sitting on the couch where I had seen the figure the previous night. When you talk to my dog he gets excited and wiggles and his eyes squint and his tail wags which is what he was doing. At first I thought he was doing it to my singing but I couldn't figure out why he was staring into my bedroom. I laughed just thinking his hearing was bad or something and approached him. But he continued to ignore me and kept his eyes and attention trained to something in my room. He jumped off the couch and darted into my room playfully. I was about 10 feet from him when he did this and I followed him into my room, expecting my mom or something to have came inside but there was no one and he was still acting very playful in my room as if he were seeing something or being spoken to. I ended up taking him back to his house outside a couple days later after he chewed up a bunch of my things while I was gone.

A couple weeks later, which is roughly two months ago the first thing happened where I felt truly threatened. I was coming down the hall when I heard a very violent dog bark/growl. Like a short burst of sound as a warning that I was in trouble. I stopped in the hall frozen in fear. Did a dog get into my house and was about to attack? Once the sound had sank in and registered I realized I had no clue from which direction it came. It felt like a surrounding sound instead of a pinpointed location. I stood in the bathroom looking back down the hall for a dog to come at me. My heart was racing, I was sweating but I was also freezing, I made an aggressive run into the kitchen and living room hoping to catch the dog off guard and reverse the dominance in the room and hopefully scare the dog off. But there was nothing, just a growing fear and feeling colder and colder. By the time I reached my bedroom the cold was almost painful and I felt like I was surrounded and just waited for something to attack. I had to get out of the house, I grabbed my work clothes and arrived several hours early and everyone that knew me commented on how visibly shaken up I was. They noticed the goosebumps and cold chills and how I was shaky. I explained what happened, my sister who works with me suggested that me seeing a dog and hearing one meant that whatever was now happening in the house was demonic. It was taking the form of something familiar (my dog) maybe trying to convince me that it was okay to approach it. Was I being tricked? I wasn't sure what was happening. That was the last really big thing that had happened but there has always been this constant feeling and weird sounds that I'm just not convinced are 'old trailer sounds'. I don't know what to expect next, if anything. But I've heard of you and I hope you can help me out in any way you can. I'm not trying to make any assumptions or conclusions anymore. That's why I'm contacting you. What started as simple weird things has got to where I have felt really threatened. It's not an everyday thing, but it's happened and continues to happen often enough to where I'm certain I need to know what is happening.

This sounds very much like a demonic case and the very unsettling way that these inhuman agents can work. There will be more on this influence later. Now let's look at some more cases that illustrate the nature of high strangeness. The following case file is an account of a strange encounter that has happened to the authors of this book.

Personal Case File

Brandon Hudgens

My experiences have given me the ability to continually make new connections. In the beginning of my paranormal career I unwittingly tried to limit my sight and focus. Once these new connections began to take shape, I learned that as paranormal investigators we need to have an open yet objective mind. It is good to have personal theories but always question and continue to test those theories.

I want to share with you one particular experience that broadened my mind and forced me into a situation where I had to question what type of investigator I was going to be. The experience that I am about to share was one that helped mold me into the investigator I am today. By sharing this I hope that you, as an investigator, will see the benefit of questioning your theories and methods.

In March of 2012 Dennis and I had our very first case with our newly formed group CSPRI Inc. Not only was this a monumental case for CSPRI Inc because it was our first as a newly formed group, but the client was a popular place of business. We had to make a great impression. By the end of the night I do think that we did just that. I want to share my experience on this night, for it is one that changed me as a paranormal investigator.

The claims, to us, seemed harmless enough. They claimed to hear voices when they were alone, see shadows, and have an overall eerie feeling. Generally I would take every precaution when I approach a case, especially when the client is having a hard time. However, this case I felt that the only issues we would see would be residual in nature and that I would be okay by not taking ALL precautions. I was wrong!

The team performed the initial setup and sweeps flawlessly. I was proud of the team for acting as a cohesive unit and not needing much direction. I felt like the training that Dennis and I provided was paying off. We also had a new investigator-in-training with us and this was his very first investigation. He stepped back and listened to all of our experienced investigators and lent a hand as needed. After all of this we allowed the building to "cool down."

The investigator-in-training was a friend of mine that wanted to learn more about the paranormal. For the sake of this story we will simply call him John. John had never had an experience and overall he was simply curious. I would not say he was a non-believer; he just had never been exposed to anything paranormal in nature. That night his perspective would change completely. He would feel the effects of a very nasty entity for the first time.

So, since John was in training I wanted him with me for most of the night. Our first sweep together went smoothly. We went to work debunking some of the claims. We were successful and needed to get them verified so I decided that we should end that session. John seemed to enjoy what we were doing and I could see that his nervousness was beginning to deteriorate.

After a break and a stint at command central, it was our turn to investigate the second wing of the business. This is where all of the offices, break room, and storage are located. So, John and I decided to begin in the break room. We took base readings of temperature and EMF before we began any type of EVP work or debunking.

I decided to try something a little different this go around because I had success with it in the past. I told John just to sit, be quiet, and observe our surroundings. We did this for about ten minutes and I told John to take note while I performed an EVP session.

He stood up to walk my way and as he got to the coffee pot it started to run. Of course, John being new to this and on edge, he jumped and I would not quite say yelled out, but he did let out a small yelp. I could not help but laugh a little. When I looked his way I could see he was shaken, so I got up to check the coffee maker.

I thought that maybe it was on a timer and it just started from that. As I began to check it over, I noticed that it was switched off. This had me thinking that it may be a little more than just a timer. I switched the coffee maker to the on position and then back off and it began to shut down. We then left it alone. I wanted to see if it happened again. Of course, it never did, so we will never know what really happened. I for one just think that the switch was a little sensitive and by rocking it we just reset the switch.

After the coffee maker incident we continued with the EVP session. I performed the session as John watched and listened intently. We were about 5 minutes into the session and I began to notice that there was some sort of movement in the hallway. At first I thought that it was my just my eyes. I closed them for a few moments to try and refocus them. When I opened them again, I continued to see the shadow movement.

I continued the EVP session for another fifteen minutes as I watched the shadow move back and forth at the end of the hall. When I ended the session, I told John we were going to walk down the hall and check out the rooms at the end. I continued to watch the hallway as we moved. I noticed that the shadow movement went into the room on the right and never returned as we moved toward it. I took care to not tell John what I was seeing because I did not want to plant that seed in his mind. I wanted him to tell me if he saw anything.

There were two rooms at the end of the hallway, one to the right and one on the end. I had seen the shadow move into the one on the right. So, I told John we would just start in there. Still, I did not want to give away that I had seen anything. When we walked into the room there was a couch to the right and a desk centered on the wall to the left with chairs on either side. I told John I was going to take the chair at the desk and he could sit on the couch. John sat down and began taking in the room. I moved toward the chair on the right side of the desk. This chair happened to belong to the person whose office we were in.

As we were taking in the room I had noticed that goose bumps were forming on my left side. I really didn't put much thought into it because when I turned to that side I saw a recessed window and a vent above me. The only thing that I thought was strange was the fact that it would come and go. Right before I decided to begin an

EVP session I saw John looking at me strangely. I didn't say anything at first because I was simply trying to figure out what he was doing.

John finally asked, "Why do you keep standing up and sitting down?"

At first it confused me because I have not moved the entire time we were in there. I knew that it was dark and he was probably just trying to get used to the light, but I wanted to be sure.

"Tell me when you think I'm standing," I told him.

He waited just a moment and then said, "Now."

At this point I began to realize that I had goose bumps on my left side again. I really didn't want to make a big deal out of nothing, so I asked John to switch places with me. I wanted to really see what he was seeing.

He got up, as did I, and we switched seats. At first nothing happened. It was just a very dimly lit area. Then I began to see what he must have seen. There seemed to be a shadow shaped like a person rising up out of the chair. I focused really hard and could tell that it was not John standing up.

The shadow would rise to about the height of a person and then begin to sink back into the chair. This shadow did this several times in a row. At this point I could make a clear distinction between John and the shadow and I could see that John was beginning to look uncomfortable.

"Are you okay?" I asked

He looked my way and I could see that he was not.

"Not really. I kind of feel sick." He replied.

I told him that we were done here and we should go ahead and go outside. I began to see what was happening and I really didn't want John's first investigation to be his first demonic attack.

When we stepped in the hallway I stopped him and asked if he was feeling better. He thought about it for a second and then said, "Yeah!"

"Let's get you outside and get some soda in you." I told him.

I didn't have to say it twice. He was quickly down the stairs and out the door. When we got outside I happened to look at my watch and it read 2:45. I took a deep breath myself and walked over to Dennis and told him what had just happened.

We both then agreed that we needed to go back up stairs and face whatever was in that room. It was almost 3:00 AM, so we began to prepare ourselves for whatever this thing was.

Dennis and I made our way back to the second story of this business to investigate the office that I had recently vacated with John. When we got to the office we decided not to enter the room across from the office for a few moments. We wanted to see if we could witness anything happening in the office before we entered. We were not disappointed.

As we watched the doorway we saw a shadow move in and out of the door frame. It was almost like the shadow was just as curious of us as we were of it. The shadow continued to dance in and out of the doorway for a while, and then suddenly it stopped. That is when Dennis and I walked into the office.

When we walked in I took the chair that I sat in originally when I was with John and Dennis sat on the other side of the desk. We were both facing the couch on the wall. After settling in our chairs we were greeted by what I can only describe as a large mass that seemed to be darker than the darkness surrounding it. It was not black or shadowy; it was completely void of light.

 As we sat in the office watching this mass grow larger and larger, we could begin to see it moving toward us slowly. I attempted to take several photographs, video, and I even attempted to get EMF/temperature readings off of the mass. Nothing would register, however we both could see it without any issues. This was the one time that I wished we has a zero lux camera available. I have always wondered if it would have captured what we were seeing.

Now the mass had slowly made its way to Dennis. Again, I was trying to get any sort of reading off of the mass that I could, but nothing would register. As it approached Dennis I could see his face wince as if he were in pain. Suddenly, the mass darted against the wall we were facing and Dennis just looked at me with astonishment written on his face. It wasn't until we were on our way home that he told me what had happened. I will get to that at the end of the story. Now this mass began to grow even more. I would say it was about eight feet tall and about six or seven feet wide now. I was still amazed at what we were seeing and I was continually trying to capture it on our devices. This is when I noticed that there was a red dot on the wall. Considering I was trying to capture this mass I did not want any contamination to contend with. I tried my best to find the source of the red light and I never could. Of course, Dennis had no clue what I was doing. He was busy staring at the wall. As I was about to give up Dennis spoke.

"Do you see those two red dots on the wall?" He asked.

I replied, "No I only see one."

At that time I saw the source of the red dot. At that moment I no longer saw a mass of darkness, I saw the face of evil. Whatever we were facing in that doctors office was real. The red dots were not created by anything in the room, they were the eyes of this thing.The eyes were coming from the mist, and within the mist was a face unlike any I had ever seen. I instantly became mesmerized.

Before I explain what I saw I want to explain what had happened to me. It is almost like this thing moved deep into my subconscious and removed all happiness from me. I instantly became depressed. I was never afraid or lonely only depressed. I felt like I could have cried until the end of time and the desperation would never go away. I instantly began reciting the Lord's Prayer in my mind and the feeling began to fade. That is when I noticed the face disappeared.

This face was unlike anything I would have ever expected to see. I will attempt to explain it to the best of my ability. It had a human head that was bald. The ears seemed a little larger than a normal human though. Behind the faint red glow were eyes black as the void it had created in the room. Now, there are two distinct features that still haunt me to this day. Where the mouth and nose should have been was the snout of a horse and on top of the head were two horns like that of a ram.

I had never in my life witnessed anything so evil in my life. As the time moved forward we noticed that the mass was beginning to shrink. Honestly, I was thankful for that. I was still depressed, though not as bad as when I was attacked. Dennis and I finally decided that we had, had enough and rebuked the presence while I turned on all of the lights. I had never been so thankful for light as I was at that moment.

When Dennis and I rejoined the others, they knew something was wrong. We never said anything and just told them that it was time to stop and pack up the equipment.

After everything was packed away everyone gathered around. That is when Dennis and I began to tell them about what we experienced. After talking I noticed that the sun was beginning to peak around the horizon and I knew that we needed to perform our location blessing. The cleansing was performed and a prayer of protection was said. I told the client that we would be more than willing to help if any future action was needed and we parted ways.

On the way home I asked Dennis what happened to him when the mist moved in toward him. His answer did not surprise me. He told me about how he saw the mist moving in and thought that it was strange. As it moved in he could feel the area getting cooler and what felt like static charge building. When the mist finally touched him he said it felt almost as if he were having a heart attack. His breathing shortened and there was a pain in his chest. He told me that there was one thing that popped in his head. He never uttered a word but he said that the phrase, *Greater is he in me than he is in the world*. At that moment, the mist moved away from him and against the wall.

I can say, without a shadow of doubt, we ran into a demon that night. It was not my first run in with a demon, but it was the first time I was attacked. I felt the effects of that attack for almost a week. It was a horrible thing to go through.

I now realized that that night I may have felt prepared, but I let my guard down. I hope that this can be a lesson to anyone trying to investigate the paranormal. Never let your guard down, EVER.

Chapter Three

Stranger Still

Truth is stranger than fiction, but it is because Fiction is obliged to stick to possibilities; Truth isn't.

Mark Twain

The world around us, the very Universe itself, is a vast thing of the unknown. It is, of course, the essence of our existence and its very nature is the mysterious. It holds its secrets well, but from time to time, if we are lucky or persistent, or both, it will show us some of its secrets. We who are fascinated by these mysteries are touched to the heart of our souls by their allure. It is a trumpet call to the truly adventurous that they can never deny. Let us now turn our attention to just a few of these mysteries that call to us in our present time. The following are perfect examples of what we know as High Strangeness, but never forget, once you start looking into the paranormal it just might start looking back at you.

Cryptozoology

Cryptozoology has been defined as the study of hidden animals. Basically, it is a scientific endeavor to uncover animals that have not been proven to exist or have been considered extinct. Many times throughout our known history people have told tales of strange creatures that they have come across on their journeys. Sometimes these tales become things of legend, or people simply shrug it off as only a myth. Other times these myths are found to be true. I want to discuss these creatures of former myth and legend.

The first former cryptid we want to discuss is one of our favorites, the platypus. Early settlers to Australia began to talk about a strange furry creature that had the tail of a beaver, bill of a duck, and webbed feet. The myth grew even more when reports came that it looked like a mammal but it laid eggs and that it was venomous. Many esteemed scientist deemed that this creature did not exist. Even when one was delivered to them, dead of course, they claimed that it was an elaborate hoax, that all of the parts were skillfully sewn together. It was not until a few years later that scientist actually agreed that the platypus existed.

Another great former cryptid is the mountain gorilla of east Africa. Tales of "ape-men" had been floating around for centuries between the tribes in that area. The tales were of savage hairy beasts that would kill and kidnap. Andrew Battel, a 16th Century English explorer, told tales of man sized apes coming into his camp at night. In the 19th Century another explorer, Du Chaillu, would tell tales of violent creatures that lived in the jungles. All of these accounts were considered tales and nothing else. Finally, in 1902 Captain Robert von Beringe, a German officer, shot and killed one of these mythical creatures. He brought it back to Europe and we were introduced to a cryptid that had been around for centuries. We could probably say with confidence that one of the most famous of the former cryptids is the giant squid. There have been tales circulating since ancient times about this creature. True, that most of the tales are probably myths, we do not think that a squid actually ate a ship. These legends continued until the late 1800s when carcasses began to wash up on beaches in Canada. This proved to the world that these creatures were real. Still, it was not until the 21st Century that one was captured alive on camera. There is not much known about the giant squid, but one thing is for sure, they are real.

We could go on and on with many examples of former cryptids, but that is for another time. Our point is this; do not ever discount the cryptids that we have today as being myth. We may only be one step away from myth becoming reality.

The Men and Women In Black

In the records of High Strangeness, one subject alone stands for the highest of High Strangeness and that is the existence of the infamous, Men In Black. Of course I'm not talking about the comic book characters from the movies of the same name, but a presence and association of evil that has haunted mankind, down through the ages. The men in black (MIB), yes even the Women In Black (WIB), have a very long history indeed. The MIB have been spoken of as being seen on the road to Athens during the time of Plato. There are records of these men and women being present during the great plaques of medieval times. They are even mentioned in transcripts of the Salem witchcraft trials.

Prevalent up until our time, there are many explanations sought for these very strange denizens of the paranormal. Some think they are alien in origin, while it is thought by others that they are agents of a secret unknown section of the government. They are considered by some to be representatives of the demonic. Whatever they maybe, they give the effect of something that does not belong in the world of mankind.

These beings are sometimes connected to Ufology, but they also encompass many other aspects of the supernatural as well. We have over the years researched as much as possible into the many stories and accounts of these odd and very unsettling agents who show up to question and intimidate witnesses to UFOs, cryptid sightings, and various other paranormal activities.

Although not as prevalent as the MIB, there are reports of Women In Black as well. It is a fascinating and strange study of the unknown and the unexplained elements of our world. We invite you to look into it for yourself. However, take special care what you say or who you say it to. Or perhaps late one night, there may be a knock at your door and you too may be visited by the minions of darkness known as The Men in Black.

BEK -- The Black Eyed Kids

Imagine this if you will....

The night has just fallen, you are about to settle down for the evening and watch a movie or relax, when suddenly, there is a knock at the door. You get up and gaze through the peephole and you see that it is just some kids on your porch. You open the door and there are three kids standing there. They are all wearing hoodies and they range in age from ten to maybe fourteen. When you answer the door the seemingly oldest kid, closest to you, begins to insist, not ask, that they be invited in and allowed to use your phone. That is when an unreasonable fear begins to slowly take hold of you and you deeply sense that something is very wrong and things definitely just don't "feel right." You then begin to look closer and see that all three of the children before you have completely black eyes. Not just the irises, but there is no white showing at all. Furthermore, the blackness of those eyes appears to be endless and soulless. That is when the fear grips you ever more tightly, you begin to panic, and slam and lock the door. You find it hard to breath and stay calm. After slamming the door the knocking begins again. You then tell yourself that there is no way on earth you are going to open your door and face those "things" again. Soon, after some time the knocking will cease. Nevertheless, you hide in your own house till dawn. You, like many others, have just faced The Black Eyed Kids. Who are they? What are they? Researchers have been asking those questions since the reports of these encounters began a few years ago. There is very valid evidence that this is not a new experience, but something that may have been going on for many centuries.

There are theories that state the BEK are vampire like beings, some think that they may be strange alien hybrids of some sort, and Demonologists speculate that they are demonic in nature. One must admit that the fear and dread they generate, does sound very much like the forces of the demonic. There are almost no existent reports of what happens if someone lets these BEKs into their home. Let us hope no one ever finds out. Perhaps maybe we really don't want to know...wait...is that someone at your door?

The Midnight Game

The authors are not in the business of giving how-to instructions on how to use the instruments of evil. So, no instructions will be given here on how to play this so called game. Many students of demonology consider The Midnight Game simply a new way in the old practices of raising demons. We don't want your blood on our hands, so we will leave it up to you if you wish to pursue this subject and we highly urge you not to pursue it. The Midnight Game and its many variations, has a following in certain internet forums. Young people are always looking for excitement, ways to impress the other sex, or simply some way to test their courage in front of their friends. These are generally accomplished by testing the line between good and evil, breaking the law, or placing yourself in danger, perceived or otherwise. Ouija boards, evoking Bloody Mary, or getting a Demon to stalk you are some of the ways that we have seen the young adults put themselves in danger and that is what this game is all about.

You call up a demon at a certain time and he will begin to stalk you as you play the "game" with him. Will you win or will he?

However, if Demonologists are correct, the Demon has nothing to lose. You on the other hand, may lose everything. There are reports of cases where young people have gone insane, after playing this game and in other cases they commit suicide with no outward signs of depression. Their very lives, in the playing of this game are at stake.

Are you really willing to risk everything for a little excitement?

Sure, tell yourself that it is just a game. That may be all it is for you, but for evil spirits on the side of darkness, it is not a game at all. These evil spirits have been known to play for keeps and they never, ever, play fair.

The "Thin Man" and The Rake

The Rake and the so called "Thin Man" are said to so closely resemble each other. They could almost be one and the same. The "Thin Man" is actually the brainchild of one man, but Rakes are said to be the personification of an actual Demon. The Rake has been documented from medieval times. The main difference between the entity known as the "Thin Man" and the Rake is that the "Thin Man" has tentacles (sounds a little like Lovecraft doesn't it), whereas the Rake has unusually long arms with very long claws, hence the rake like description. Both, however, are said to be supernatural stalkers, especially of children or anyone, for that matter, who gets in their way. Demonologists think that the Rake is very real. The "Thin Man," on the other hand, is just a figment of one man's imagination, or is he?

Paranormal Investigators are seeing more and more reports on a "Thin Man" like being that people are encountering. These people who never had any knowledge of the Internet forums that supposedly gave birth to the "Thin Man" are now reporting sightings of this very being. Those who study Demonology are beginning to wonder if this image is now being used by the Demonic to foster negative and fearful feelings in their victims. This is something that demons have been well known to thrive on in the past. So, is the "Thin Man" now a real entity? Is the Rake waiting out there somewhere in the shadows? Let us hope that you never have to find out.

The Black Stick Men

There have been those who have reported strange encounters with black, shadow like beings, who are said to be extremely long and incredibly thin creatures that are huge and mechanical like in their movements. There have also been films released to social media supposedly taken by people who have had run-ins with these other worldly creatures. In these videos, fantastically large and weird beings are seen stalking through parks and climbing up the side of high rise buildings. They resemble strange stick like figures on a gigantic scale. Are these creatures from another weird dimension? Are they figments of human imagination? Or, are they simply the product of manipulated computer programs? You must be the judge of that, but meanwhile when you find yourself in the park after sundown, be sure to watch your back.

The Black Knight Satellite

The legend of what is now known as the Black Knight Satellite began many years ago. The legend began during 1950s and 60s. It was a time in our civilization when man began to look toward the stars. It has been rumored to be continually rotating this planet and it is also said to travel in a tight orbit, an orbit that is far past those of commercial and military satellites. Agencies, whose task it is to monitor all space debris, are said to pick it up on radar grids from time to time and when they do, it is a brief encounter with a shadow like, space phantom. That encounter is always a brief one as it is always quickly gone. Even astronauts on the International Space Station have reported seeing this object circling the Earth. It is reported by some that although its orbit is continuous, it also is a fluctuating one that is ever changing in its trajectory. If this is true, then this strange craft would have to be under the control of some sort of intelligence. Has this mysterious visitor been circling this planet since before mankind ever supposedly launched anything into space? Is the Black Knight Satellite really there or is it just an echo in the void or just a story of the space age? Is it simply a ghost out there, in the eternal blackness? If it does exist, is it military, is it from this earth, or from somewhere else completely? There are even some that believe the ancient Mayans built a craft that could escape Earth's gravitational field and this is that craft. Could it be a remnant of ancient astronauts? We challenge you to look at the evidence in research and come to your own conclusion, and if you do, you must bear in mind this question. If the Black Knight Satellite really is orbiting over your head, why is it there?

Rougarou, Dogmen, Werewolves, and The Wendigo.

A legendary creature that is said to haunt the bayous of the American south is the monster known as the rougarou, the terrifying boogeyman of the swamps. The rougarou is sometimes called the Loup Garou. He has an interesting characteristic in common with his cousin the wendigo. They both are sometimes described as being spirits of the land that under certain circumstances can possess human beings to carry out their attacks.

There is another interesting thing about the rougarou, it is also often described as looking an awful lot like Bigfoot or a werewolf. This has been noted in two very famous cases in the South; The Honey Island Swamp Monster and the Fouke Monster (The Legend of Boggy Creek).

The Wendigo, a very well known Native American Indian legend found in the folklore and tradition of many tribes, is also described sometimes as a Bigfoot type Monster as well.

Could they all possibly be one and the same? Described differently by different eyewitnesses?

Another interesting thing about the rougarou and the wendigo is that when someone is possessed by either of these entities that person, it is said, becomes a cannibal. It desires only human flesh.

We also have the dogmen and werewolves often reported throughout Michigan, Indiana, and other mid-western states. Could they also be the same creature? After interviewing several witnesses to monster activity, I have noted one definite thing we as researchers should keep in mind. Fear can often alter your perception of things. An encounter of this nature would definitely be fearful. So, described testimonies in these cases need to be gone over thoroughly to make sure it is substantial enough to hold up to the true case of what actually happened. That of course is the reason why real monster hunters, a.k.a. Cryptid Researchers, are out there. No hill or cave or rocky trail will keep them from the pursuit of the truth.

The Skin Walkers

The legend of the skin-walker is very prevalent in the South Western United States, especially among the Navaho and Hopi tribes. However, it is also found in many other connected cultures and tribes as well.

Whether the Skin Walker is called brujo, diablero, medicine man, shaman, or even wendigo, as it is known to the Northern Native American Tribes, a skin-walker is simply a shape shifter. That is a man, or woman, who by the means of some dark magic, can put on the personification of and transform into another being other than themselves. In other words, they can step over into another reality. It is then that they can perform spells, curses and other such black magic upon their enemies, in order to harm them, their families, or possessions in some way. These beings are feared and avoided by Native Americans, who will rarely even talk about them. They believe to talk about skin-walkers is to draw their attention to you and then you would definitely have a problem of what some would call "bad medicine."

There have been many reports about encounters with these evil witches. People have been known to be haunted by these creatures most of their lives. There is one story that came across our desk of a family that moved into a small ranch. Their livestock began to be attacked on an almost nightly basis. A strange red light would be often seen near the barn when their livestock was being attacked. The husband had rock salt blessed by a priest and then he loaded that salt in a shot gun shell. The next time the red light appeared he shot at it with the rock salt shot. After he fired he heard a very loud inhuman scream. He said that the sound was not even animalistic. He had a very difficult time explaining it. The next day he walked out to the spot where he saw the red light that he shot and found some fur, a bunch of black crow feathers, blood, but nothing else. The attacks on his livestock ceased immediately from that time on. He believed without a doubt, that the blessed rock salt took care of the brujo or skin-walker. It would be very wise to bear this in mind should you find yourself one dark night on a lonely road. There are still places out there, in God forsaken areas, where weird things can and do happen.

You might want to pack a little blessed salt in your gear…just in case.

Angel Hair

Angel hair is the name of a strange substance that has been reported to fall from the sky worldwide. It is said to be of an almost ethereal composition. In many instances it is described as being an off white color and semi transparent in nature. Samples have been collected, but they quickly dissolve without leaving any residue behind. Some speculate that it is the substance left behind by UFOs. Others think it is either an unknown type of air pollution or a naturally occurring airborne life form of some kind that is created or formed either in the atmosphere of the Earth or somewhere in the darkness of outer space.

Whatever it may be, it has a bizarre, almost paranormal make up. Angel hair has been reported for many years. It was one of the very first paranormal things that Dennis remembers hearing about in his childhood. It was thought back then, that it might be some kind of fallout from nuclear blast tests. There have been rare reports of people getting sick after handling Angel Hair or of being in close proximity to it. So what is Angel Hair really?

It is definitely an unknown X factor that still has a lot of researchers stumped. More might perhaps be learned if we could just keep the samples from disappearing into the unknown.

Bigfoot / Yeti

This creature is probably the most famous of all of the paranormal creatures that we study. Many books have been written about Bigfoot, Yeti, Sasquatch, or the numerous other names this creature is known by throughout most of the world. The shadow of Sasquatch looms large in the folklore of many cultures, but does he really exist? We have heard from many people who believe so. Many who claim encounters with this being. We even have our own experiences to relate.

Bigfoot -- Dennis' Story

My first Sasquatch Investigation...

Well over twenty years ago, when I was a much younger man, I had the reputation among my coworkers of someone who was well acquainted with anything of a bizarre and supernatural nature. My fellow coworkers, of whom there were several thousand, would often seek me out to tell me of the strange things that they had heard or the strange experiences that they or their friends had happen to them. On one such occasion one particular fellow whom I had not been acquainted with, as he was fairly new, told me of a very strange encounter that he and his girl friend had a few weeks prior. I told him that I would meet him and his lady friend a few days later at a nearby restaurant. The following is the story they told me of their strange incident.

They had been parked one autumn night on a very secluded lover's lane, which was a dirt road out in the country. It was what we always called a turnaround road. That means it was a dead end and had a circular turn around at the end to use when you wanted to leave. They of course where there engaging in the business of lovers on a lover's lane. That is when, just like in a horror movie, the girl heard something or someone walking in the thick woods that surrounded them. The fellow got angry at the thought of someone spying on them. He grabbed his flashlight and got out to confront whoever it was. Well the flashlight, as it turned out, had dead batteries. So, he ended up trying to see who was out there in those dark woods with only the light of the stars on a moonless night. Immediately he saw a movement off to his left where the dead-end road sign was planted into the ground. He took a few steps and stopped in his tracks, as something huge emerged before him. It was a very big shadow, darker than the darkness behind it. He was so startled at the sight that for a moment he was paralyzed. It stood up next to the road sign and towered over it. This was a sign that I later measured at almost seven feet in height. Although the thing at the time was moving away from him, he wasn't taking any chances. He turned and hightailed it back to the car, a Volkswagen Beetle. As he got behind the wheel in this panicked state, his girlfriend also began to freak out, because she had never seen him like this before. Then they both could hear footsteps of this thing bounding closer. The guy quickly cranked the VW and as he was putting it in gear, they felt a bump and the rear end of the car slowly left the ground for a second and the vehicle was then given a slight shove. As they hit the ground the wheels were moving in fast forward and for a minute the fellow had to fight to gain control of the car. Nevertheless, they got out of there, vowing never to go back there again. Which as far as we know, after that unsettling experience, they never did.

After interviewing this couple, hearing and seeing the fear still evident in their voices and eyes, I definitely had to go to the place and investigate it for myself. There was one more thing they both mentioned about that night. They both noted a very bad smell. It was a strong odor they said of something dead or of something like sulfur. Of course I found the place, but the trail of the incident was over a month old and it had rained several times since the encounter took place. I looked for tracks, broken brush, but I came up empty. I measured the sign and looked around for any kind of evidence, but all I noticed was a very faint smell of what might possibly be skunk. The place was very quiet and far away from any kind of civilization.

As I had mentioned, it was a perfect lover's lane and maybe an even better hangout for a Bigfoot.

My Recent Experience...

In my 40 plus year career, in the field of paranormal research and investigation, the area of cryptozoology has always been a favorite of mine. I remember way back in the year of 1971 when I came across a book on the Yeti (abominable snowman of the Himalayas) and also an old movie which starred Peter Cushing (The Abominable Snowman), that my curiosity was aroused to the mystery of this creature and that of its North American cousin the Sasquatch (Bigfoot). I have read and researched thousands of case histories and reports that covered any and everything about the so called cryptid creatures of this world. Cryptozoology opened up a whole new fascinating area of the paranormal for me. I was already involved not only in ghosts and demonology, but ufology and earth anomalies as well. I've always been a folklorist and legend seeker who since the earliest days of my youth, has been captivated by the many mysteries of this world. The beings of cryptozoology have that tie to the mystery of the creatures that we know as monsters and monsters are known in almost every culture worldwide. These denizens of the dark and unknown are not only inhabitants of nightmares but also they can be called something very close to a racial memory, imbedded deep in the mind of mankind itself. When some friends of mine recently told me of some very strange activity that was happening very close to their home, me being me, no way was I going to turn down the opportunity to look deeper into these incidents. When my friend and colleague Brandon Hudgens and I had formed our paranormal team (Carolina Society for Paranormal

Research and Investigation Inc) a few years earlier, we had been hoping that just such a case as this would come up. About twenty years prior to this, I had looked into a report of a strange hairy creature that had been sighted on a dirt road situated in the Broadway lake area, on the outskirts of Anderson S C. (which also involved several UFO reports), so I had some experience in very similar cases. Also I had recently checked out some sightings of ABCs (alien big cats) as well.

Reports were coming in to us of strange structures in the woods and tree knockings, along with very unusual night noises, in the large tract of woods near the home of our friends in Seneca-Oconee County. Then several large foot prints were found in the woods, one that we cast was 18 inches in length. This was and still is a golden opportunity of research, too good to pass up for any of us. So I suggested to my friends that I would like to stake the area out for a few hours of daytime observation. Although I was to do this alone, I was also to keep in constant contact via walkie-talkie with my friends nearby. I set up a video camera on a tripod when I established my area of observation. I was situated very near to where the foot prints were found, as I figured this would be the perfect place for a possible sighting. I kept a constant eye on the sky as the clouds all day looked very threatening and as the summer heat was very oppressive, it was perfect weather for thunderstorms. The spot I had was very well hidden and I settled in for a long time of watching and waiting. As everything soon settled down and returned to a relative state of normalcy I began to notice something very peculiar. Every hour or so, there would come a brief period of silence. Even the birds would quit singing. It immediately gave me the feeling as though something was circling my location, in the very thick brush around me. There was also that instinctive feeling of being constantly watched. My video camera at this time began to do some crazy things. I had my reliable handy-cam that day and it did some things it had never done before or has done since. While the image was on the screen and the record button was pressed it only had a blank image. It was as if I was in extreme sunlight with it, but I wasn't. I was in the shade the whole time. The most peculiar part is that the camera worked perfectly fine after I left those woods. Also during the times of strange silence I noticed a slight fluctuation in my compass. It was ever so slight however, not dramatic at all. After about four hours I noticed the sky getting darker and some distant thunder so I knew it was time to leave. As I was packing my gear I looked to my right, deep into the brush, and I could see a patch of sunlight in a slight clearing in the bushes probably twelve yards or so distant from me. It was then that I saw a very large shadow fall swiftly across this patch of sunlight. It was not a bird and the shadow was too large to even be a dog. The shadow was even much larger than the shadow of a man would be. I immediately made for that clearing, but as I said, the brush was very thick and it took me sometime to make it to that open space and of course by then there was nothing there to see. Thunder was getting louder and I knew I had very little time before the rain and storm would break. I radioed my friends that I was on the way back in and I left the woods and got back to their house just barely about the time the storm hit. The entire stake out was very strange and I felt most of the time that I definitely was not alone out there in those woods. I see a definite future return to that area for another possible stake out, hopefully on the night of a very bright full moon. It would perhaps I think, definitely yield some very interesting results. I am most definitely looking forward to that.

Follow up...

My Most Recent Experience...

I was recently on a sasquatch night hunt in the wilds of Oconee County, with two companions. We had been walking around in the dark woods of our research area when we heard a tree knock. For those who don't know, a tree knock is just that, the sound of wood on wood. Most of the time, it is a hit on the trunk of a tree when it is thought that Bigfoot hits the tree with a limb or stick. Speculation is, that it's a form of communication between a tribe or group of sasquatch and it is also thought too that it can be a warning of some kind. We decided then that I would sit down there on a nearby log and quietly observe, while one fellow went to my right and the other guy went the left. It was their determination to return back to my location in a wide arc to hopefully flush out in my direction, what might have made that sound. It almost worked. I had a night vision scope with me and in the darkness there I would periodically scan and check my surroundings. As anyone knows who has ever used a night vision scope, it can after awhile, begin to hurt your eyes. So, it is good to give it a rest from time to time. As I was doing this, I heard a series of three tree knocks, one on each side of me and one at my back. I was beginning to wonder if I was in the middle of some kind of tree knock game, I saw a slight movement to my left. I immediately raised my scope and very briefly caught a glimpse of what looked very much like the elbow of a very hairy arm, disappearing behind a large tree. As it did so, it left a small, five foot high sapling, swaying in its path. For the record there was absolutely no wind that night, not even a slight breeze. I kept scanning every section of its direction for any movement, but there was absolutely none. It was as if it had almost supernaturally disappeared. The hair on that elbow by the way was long and a light brown or maybe what would be called "dirty blond". As anyone who has ever ventured out in the forest, far from the lights of civilization, knows, it doesn't really get much darker than that. In the wilderness, unless there's a full moon, the only light source you have is what you bring with you. To move in any kind of reasonable fashion in darkness like that, requires extreme caution and the safety of your light source. In order for someone to move that swiftly, like whatever it was I encountered, you would have to have the eyes of a cat or some kind of light. To try and do that, especially if you are wearing a costume of some kind, seems highly unlikely and darned near humanly impossible to hoax. In that kind of situation, to pull off something like that, you would almost have to have super human type powers. What appeared and disappeared before me was I can say, definitely not a human being. I still don't really know what it was I saw, but it has left me with far more questions than answers.

We suggest that for more interesting reading on the subject of Bigfoot, werewolves, dog men, and other supposed shapeshifter cryptids that you check out any of the books written by the very fine and highly esteemed Author and Researcher Linda Godfrey. Among her many books is our favorite, *American Monsters*.

Bigfoot -- Brandon's Story

When High Strangeness is being discussed, Bigfoot is a topic that comes to my mind. Ever since I was a child I had sort of a fascination with Bigfoot. I always wondered what would happen if I ever ran into one while my grandmother and I would take walks in the woods. I knew that the west coast of the US was where most of the sightings had been and where the trackers were, but never in my wildest dreams would I have thought that there would be sightings near the area I live. One day, as luck would have it, I was discussing the signs of Bigfoot habitation with a few people and near the end of the conversation they told me that they have actually seen and heard much of what we just talked about. My interest in Bigfoot increased tenfold when they told me this.

There were many points of view that night. I would get into a lot more detail of what they told me about their experiences, but I can only tell this story from my point of view. To begin, my group had decided to get a small band of people together and try to find some sort of evidence that a Bigfoot type creature was lurking in Seneca, SC. Some of our members knew someone with a lot of land that was wooded and that had a very large swamp adjacent to the property. These were just the sort of hiding places we may find a Bigfoot. We decided to have a cookout and a fun gathering before we began searching for our evidence.

We grilled hotdogs that evening. Our theory behind this is the simple fact that Bigfoot had been spotted around people camping. We thought that is there was any Bigfoot around that this may entice them. Honestly, as this story unfolds you may find that this was true.

After eating and communing with one another the owners decided to show us some areas where they saw some oddities and they also wanted us to look at the area in general. As we began to walk they would tell stories of how rocks would get thrown at them, how they found streaked mud on top of leaves eight feet in the air, they would hear strange animal noises that were not familiar.

The next day I went back out and began searching the area more closely. At the base of several of the trees I found what seemed to be deep impressions in the soil at the base of the trunk. As I studied it, it seemed like a very large footprint but it did not take any real shape or form. It was, however, still very curious.

I told the owner that I wanted to go deeper into the woods that day.

They agreed because they haven't been deep into the woods in a while and wanted to just check it out anyway. As we ventured I spied several game trails and decided to follow them for a while.

We came upon one very curious item, a hole. I know that a hole in the ground is usually not very curious but this one was. It went down, over, and out and the part of the hole that we could see was about four feet in diameter and it had a uniform circumference. I could understand that some animal could do this, but the dirt was in one nice large pile on one side of the hole only. I know that a human could not do this by hand or with remedial tools and we were too far into the woods for someone to bring large equipment. The best part is this is not the strangest thing we saw that day.

As we moved along the game trails we found what appeared to be a wooden structure. It was very large and heavy limbs that were interwoven. There is a minute chance this could have happened in nature, but not when small saplings are interwoven as well. That structure was placed there with a purpose.

After seeing several other strange structures we decided to head back to that clearing once more to try and find some sort of physical evidence. As I was walking around the clearing I saw something odd in the grass. I moved closer and began to carefully move the grass out of the way. I cleared enough grass to finally see there in front of me was the perfect indention of a heel, a very large heel. I looked around and told the person with the largest foot to carefully come over to me. I asked him to take his shoe and sock off so that I could examine it. His heel was not even close to the size of the heel I found in the ground.

I quickly told them to stop what they were doing and look for tracks in that area. I then tried to figure out why this area was good for tracks. It appeared to me that the soil in this one particular area is very soft, which is odd for South Carolina red mud. I then was curious how the heel was so deep because, me being the heaviest person there, my footprint was barely visible and I am 210 pounds. Whatever made this impression was far heavier than me.

As everyone swept the area we began to find more and more impressions. After looking at them I determined that there were two distinct sets. One set was about twelve inches long and twice as wide as a normal foot but shallow like our tracks and the other was eighteen inches long and slightly wider than a normal human foot.

After taking photos and measurements I wanted one last look and that is when I found it. I had come across a fully impressed eighteen inch footprint. Even the toes were distinguishable. We attempted to get a cast, but the mixture we used was slightly too heavy and it damaged the footprint. Sadly, we were not able to completely get the full cast of this beautiful impression.

Today we are continuing to find more trees down, more structures built, trees with the bark stripped from them from the ground to about ten feet in the air, and more impressions. We have yet to find another hole or another impression as beautiful as that full impression, but we are continuing our search for clues. It is my hope that one day when we least expect it, a very large and hairy creature will walk up on us.

I do not want to harm the creature. I simply want to study it and understand how on Earth this thing has eluded man for so long. More so, I want definitive proof that Bigfoot does indeed exist

Bigfoot / Yeti – Final Thoughts

The authors want the readers to understand that they have not decided on the existence of this very elusive creature. However, their thought is, if this creature does in fact exist, what is Sasquatch really? Where does it come from and where does it go? Where does the legend end and reality begin?

Various tribes of Native American Indians, from what we now know as the Carolinas to the Great Pacific Northwest, had over a hundred names for this creature. Did they know something we do not? Perhaps they had to live with the terror of a creature like this in the woods, or perhaps they learned to live with it peacefully or at least an uneasy truce.

One of the most perplexing questions that the authors have is why is the story of this creature found worldwide in so many diverse cultures? Are tales of creatures like this a part of our DNA? The memories of history are silent for now, until we find solid proof.

So, if late one night in the woods near your house there falls an eerie silence and you notice the moon is low on the horizon, you see a strange shadow moving across the land and you feel the eyes of something watching from the darkness. Bear in mind the story of Bigfoot and try to tell yourself...it is just a legend after all.

Areas of Anomalous Activity (The AAA)

Skinwalker (Bigelow) Ranch Utah, Roswell, New Mexico, Area51 Nevada, Point Pleasant, W.Virginia, Dulce, New Mexico, and San Luis Valley, Colorado.

The above list of famous places is known areas of anomalous activity, but areas of this type, can be found anywhere, at any time. Most of the areas mentioned above are along the 37th parallel of the United States. Oddly enough, a very large amount of high strangeness is recorded along this line. It is thought that many ley lines, the naturally and invisible occurring electromagnetic lines of the Earth, run also along this parallel. Any place in close proximity to these areas and these lines is a good candidate for strange and anomalous activity. Anything from UFOs, ghosts, and earth lights to Bigfoot sightings are often reported.

As researchers and investigators (most of the time you really can't be one without the other) we should take important note of this, especially where these lines may cross. They are definite areas of a high probability for high strangeness. A lot of researchers feel that these areas are also prime places for the supposed occurrence of portal activity.

One example is the Bigelow (Skinwalker) Ranch in Utah. It has been reported to host anomalous lights, UFOs, sightings of strange monster type creatures, and supposed portals that have also been seen. Another example is the San Luis Valley in Colorado, which has been the research area of paranormal investigator and author Chris O'Brian. In his very good book on the subject *The Mysterious Valley*, he records many accounts of not only UFOs and cattle mutilations, but other weird and bizarre occurrences. Several books have been written about the incidents of high strangeness that occur in this location on what is said to be a regular basis. The same can also be said for all the other places mentioned here. There are some pretty strange places out there in our strange universe. We must continue to keep our eyes open to the weird possibilities that may be there as well.

Mothman

Of course we have all heard what happened in Point Pleasant, West Virginia many years ago and the experiences of those who encountered the legendary mothman. It is a story immortalized in the Hollywood movie *The Mothman Prophecies* and in the writings of the equally legendary, John Keel. It is a place and time to this day, that is unrivaled in the annals of the paranormal.

The mothman for those who don't know, is a supposed humanoid type creature that as described, hasn't much of a neck, stands between 6 and 8 foot tall and has glowing red eyes and huge moth like wings. It is said that these creatures can take off vertically and can out fly panic stricken drivers. However, it is well known that the mysterious mothman is not strictly an inhabitant of West Virginia, but he has also been sighted in many places worldwide.

In a recent case that was brought to our attention there was a sighting in northeastern Georgia not far from the state line of South Carolina. The mothman also has a counter part in Great Britain, where he is known as the Owl Man. If there were only one symbol of what we know as High Strangeness, it would be the mothman, most definitely. This entity is thought by many to be a harbinger of death, destruction, and evil. There are others who think he comes from some strange dimension or reality. Still, other researchers think it may be an alien hybrid of some kind or a secret government experiment gone wrong. Whatever he may be, if he really exists, he does seem to foretell disaster on occasion. The most infamous case in the authors' part of the world is the collapse of the Silver Bridge in Point Pleasant.

One fact that we know about the moth and the owl is that they both play roles in superstition that are related many times to warnings of death and bad happenings. Furthermore, the owl is a symbol of occult knowledge and forbidden teachings. The owl also is directly associated with the Goddess Athena, the ancient deity of wisdom. The moth in many cultures is a symbol of spirituality and the dead.

The reports and sightings of mothman have not slowed down by any means. There are even other cases of humanoid type flying creatures that are supposedly seen being reported as well. Are they citizens of some other worldly existence, wanderers from a parallel universe, just passing through, or the product and offspring of dabblers in the occult who may have opened doorways that were best left closed? Stranger things have happened they say. So, if on your way home some dark night, you should happen to hear large wings flapping over head, it may be best to stay your course and get where you are going as quickly as possible. Oh, and whatever you do…don't look up.

UFO -- Unidentified Flying Objects

There are of course thousands of books, movies and documentaries that have been done concerning the subject of UFOs and its related studies, such as crashes and abductions. It is the one subject alone that stands upon the mountain top of High Strangeness. It is a field without a doubt that has been used and misused by many governments and greatly misunderstood, by many people.

Most of the time, what is thought to be unidentified flying objects (UFOs) and unidentified submerged objects (USOs) are usually things that are simply misidentified. In most of these cases, it is just what the believer really wants to believe. However, what about that 10% that experts say is an unknown factor? This is a very deep and very broad study and we encourage you to look into it even more.

On a good cool clear night, have your own sky-watch with some friends to help you. Besides satellites, low and high flying airplanes, and drones you never know what you may see. The sad fact of our modern time is that we seldom pay enough attention to what is overhead, unlike our ancient ancestors who were avid sky watchers.

So, are we really being visited by Aliens? Are they kidnapping us and performing weird experiments on us? Are they really mutilating people and cattle? The jury is still out and will remain so, until true first contact is made or irrefutable evidence is found or released to the population. There is even, some say a direct connection with the demonic and UFOs. Yes, Ufology is one of the strangest of studies and one of the most intriguing.

To look up at night into the vast unknown is to look into eternity. Of all the uncountable stars and their systems and planets out there, ask yourself truthfully, how could we really be alone? Keep looking up, but don't forget, who knows what, may be looking back.

Hellhounds

It has often been stated by Demonologists that the Demonic can take on any form. This would also include the Dogs of Damnation also known as Hell Hounds. First, let's look at the legendary side of this subject. To actually see a hell hound is supposed to mean your death or the death of someone you know and it said that the demise of that person will not be a very good way to go. In short a very horrible death awaits the witness of a hell hound, especially if you should look into its eyes, which blaze like the fires of hell itself. The hell hound is often described as a huge black dog that is a terrible sight to see, ugly and completely supernatural in its unnatural composition. It, of course, has the strong smell of sulfur, or what we call brimstone, always about it. Furthermore, it is said that the Devil always sends his pets after the highest of sinners to collect their souls. The only true safe place to hide from them is consecrated ground or inside an unbroken circle of blessed salt.

The howl of these unearthly creatures is said to freeze the blood and turn the bravest of hearts to stone. It is said that these hounds frequent murder sites, the outside of graveyards, and of course crossroads. Crossroads are also the favorite haunt of evil witches and the Devil and his demons. As a precursor of death and disaster, the Hounds of Hell loom large in legend and folklore. That is the legend, but is it true?

There seem to be some points that ring right, as with all legends. The reports that usually come in now, in our day and time, are just often brief glimpses and the sounds of hell hounds. These brief sightings are often accompanied by strong feelings of extreme fear.

Sometimes they are supposedly spotted alone and sometimes they run in packs. There is a case in Southern California of a pack seen by several witnesses. They were said to have attacked a man's car. The man saw them do a lot of damage to his vehicle in the driveway. He waited till they were gone to inspect their handiwork. That is probably why he survived the incident. He said the smell of sulfur hung in the air for days. He also said after the incident that he was thinking of attending Church on a more regular basis.

More often than not, Hell Hounds are only heard and remain invisible during their attacks. They are said to run a course around and around the home of the doomed that they have come to collect. Never giving up the hunt of their prey until they get what or shall we say who, they have come for. Let's hope that shall never be your fate or that you should ever hear the Hounds of Hell on the hunt, howling in the night.

It is said that Hell Hounds run with The Devil when he rides out on The Wild Hunt!

The Wild Hunt

Some believe that the dogs of The Wild Hunt are the hunting hounds of Odin. It is told that on dark, windy, stormy nights that the Viking God Odin and his Berserkers and Valkyries ride forth on their hunt. Odin is also called by another name as well, Herne the Hunter, the Great Horned One. Others believe that it is Old Scratch himself, the Devil, which is riding out with his demons and hell hounds seeking wayward souls that have gone astray.

Many cases tell of these apparitions being seen and heard in the stormy skies at night or seen riding down roads and rushing with the wind across barren fields, hellbent for leather. In the southwestern United States this legend is known as The Ghost Riders. The Ghost Riders are the spirits of damned and doomed men forever forced to ride with the Devil's herd, across the endless skies.

The wild hunt it is said is especially fond of snatching children and young adults. To ride once with the hunt is to ride forever. These poor souls are doomed to ride till doomsday. More often than not the wild hunt is heard, but seldom seen. On the rare occasion when The Wild Ride is seen, it is thought by many to be a harbinger of evil times to come.

There was a report from the British Isles a few years ago of a man being found dead on a country road not far from the moors. He was found on the muddy dirt road the morning after an autumn storm. They said he had a terrible look of fear on his face and the hoof prints of horses all about him. There were no horses in the vicinity of the immediate area.

Did he meet The Wild Hunt on that lonely road? We may never know for sure, but if late one stormy night you think you hear what sounds like hoof beats close behind, remember, it's just the wind...or is it?

The Banshee

In the records of Celtic folklore, one entity stands alone as one of the most frightening of all and that is the fabled Banshee. Is it a woeful spirit of death, a haunting wraith attached to certain families or perhaps an elemental being from the mists of time and the long ago days of forgotten gods? Or, is it simply a fireside story of legend? Who or what the Banshee really is remains an unanswered question for many of us in the paranormal field. However, in Scotland and Ireland the Banshee is far from just folktales and superstition. It is for many who have encountered it, a very real elemental force to be reckoned with. Even the very sound of the Banshee is to be feared and seeing one may very well lead to your doom. It is said that to hear the soft far away crying of the Banshee means that a close kin will soon die. To hear the nearby loud wailing moan of the keening Banshee means the death is your own. When one sees a Banshee washing bloody clothes, it is thought that this signifies death by accident, murder, or on the battlefield. There are certain families whose surnames begin with an O or a Mc that are said to have a tradition of a family Banshee. For them the wailing Banshee is always a warning that there will soon be a vacant place in the family. When Dennis' grandfather Carroll died, there were said to be some in the immediate family several days before his demise, which had heard the far off sound of a woman crying, but could never find the source. Those of Scot-Irish blood are said to be rather attuned to these otherworldly types of manifestations, as the Celtic people are known to respect the things of the unseen. So, let's hope if you have a little Celtic blood in you that the Banshee never pays you a visit. Is the Banshee real? Many say she is, let us hope we never really find out.

La Lechuza

La Lechuza is Spanish for "The Owl." Bird Woman is another of her names. La Lechuza is a well known demonic entity feared by the Hispanic population of the American southwest and Mexico.

Also known as the Owl Witch or Owl Woman she is said to be a dark brujo or bruja who shape shifts into a human sized owl-like demon bird, with the face of a woman. She is reported to hunt children and is a stealer of souls that uses her strange calling sound to draw her prey to her. She is said to inhabit vacant and desolate places.

La Lechuza lies in wait for anyone foolish enough to wander into these somewhat haunted areas. When these unsuspecting victims do wander in her domain, she then devours them. It is thought by some, that she can lure her victims to her by the aid of black witchcraft and sorcery. It is also said that she can be most active at certain holidays, such as, a little before and after the Day of The Dead.

There are certain charms that are said to be effective against her, such as the holy wafer, holy water, blessed salt, prayers, and a small piece of iron carried in the pocket, such as a nail. However, they say the best thing is to try to avoid her at all costs by staying away from known places where she has been seen. It is told that in able to destroy La Lechuza, she must be shot with a bullet that has a cross cut on the end of the head. The old timers will tell you that the best protection of all from La Lechuza is to lead as good and holy life as possible. For they say that she hates anything or anyone who has goodness about them.

Santa Muerte

Also known as The Cult of Death, it is said to have over a million followers. Its patron Saint is a skeleton image of what seems to be the Virgin Mary. It is also called Our Lady of the Holy Death. Santa Muerte is venerated as a patron Saint of prostitutes, drug users, criminals, and members of the Mexican drug cartels. The skewed religion that surrounds this cult is influenced heavily by Catholic and Voodoo traditions, with a little of the regular black witchcraft and the Satanic thrown in for good measure. It is said too, that adherents of this belief, venerate death and see it as a means to a justifiable end. Some followers even believe that Santa Muerte makes them impervious to knives and bullets. Their belief too is, that to die gloriously is to die well.

La Llorona

La Llorona or the Weeping Woman may also be called The Wailing Woman. Just as La Lechuza is the American version of the Greek Harpy, La Llorona is the Hispanic equivalent of the Irish Banshee. She is supposedly the vengeful ghost of a woman who committed suicide after drowning her children. Her cry, it is told, is always an omen of death. She is said to haunt rivers, waterways, and of course children. In short, she is attempting to seek out your children, to replace the ones that she murdered. Like any evil spirit she has ways to lure and trap her prey and can also be driven off by holy objects and prayers.

There is a story of a family's encounter one night by a river. A husband and wife with their two children were walking by the riverside one night on their way home. They noticed that the kids, who were lagging behind and had been chattering away, suddenly went silent. The mother looked back to see her children stopped by the water's edge standing with a woman who was crying and veiled in the shadows. She quickly rushed over, grabbed the children, and she and her husband fled with them into the night. Looking back, they could see La Llorona quickly closing in behind them. The chase finally ended in the cemetery of a nearby church.

After finding that the Wailing Woman had vanished and was no longer giving chase, the husband and wife breathed a justified sigh of relief. Then they remembered that evil spirits are supposedly unable to walk on consecrated ground, such as that of a church or graveyard. It was a very narrow escape indeed. So, if you find yourself by the water one night, keep an even closer eye on those kids, because after all, you don't want to end up like La Llorona, with something to cry about.

El Chupacabra

El Chupacabra is Spanish for the goat sucker, but he is known to have a taste for a lot more than just goats. Like most beasts of prey that tears and rips up their victims, this vampire like cryptid is only interested in blood. Most prevalent in the South Western United States and Mexico, the Chupacabra is also known deep into Central and South America as well. There have even been sightings of El Chupacabra in Puerto Rico. Unlike the vampire bat, this creature is supposed to be far more destructive. Whereas the vampire bat leads a more parasitic life, the Chupacabra is a destroyer of livestock and people's livelihood. Although it preys mostly on sheep, goats and small cattle, he has been known, they say, to kill dogs and attack people. Some think if he really does exist, he may be a hybrid between a coyote or wolf, with a domestic dog. But based on eyewitness reports, those who encounter him say he is far from canine in appearance.

The resemblance they say is more like that of a kangaroo than anything else. That is, a monster looking kangaroo. He is said to have a lizard like ridge down his back, large claws and vampire-like fangs. Some say he can hop or leap at great bounds and still others say he can supernaturally disappear. What could this creature be? Is El Chupacabra real? Is this something natural but unknown or is it from another strange realm? Perhaps after all it is only an urban myth. Whatever the case, guard well your goats.

Hecate / Lilith

Hecate and Lilith are said by some to be one and the same entity. Hecate is the legendary Queen or Goddess of Witches. Lilith is said to have been Adam's first wife, who cursed him and God, then fled forever into the shadows to become the mother of all witches, sorcerers, and evil spirits of the night. She herself now is said to be a demon or Queen of the Demons. In Jewish folklore, she is sometimes thought to take on the appearance of an owl and she is said also to haunt the lonely and desolate places of the world, lying in wait to seduce and steal human souls. Hecate is one of the names given to The Goddess revered by those who are practitioners of witchcraft and the black arts. She is sometimes called the Mother Goddess. This is why some think that they may be the same person or entity since their place in folklore and characteristics are very similar. So, when lonely winds blow across the desert at night, some say there is more in that song than just the sounds of the wind. They say this is the way that Lilith, the stealer of the soul, can call to you. Whatever the case, it might be best not to listen if she does.

Night Stalker

This unknown and unseen creature is said to initiate fear, horrible nightmares, and even physically attack its victims. There is no description for this thing, as it is invisible, there is just the pervading sense of evil that it leaves behind. There have been a few attacks in the South Western US, especially on Native American Indian reservations. Some theorize that this actually maybe the work and manifestation of a skin walker, still others think that this thing, which has been given the name of The Night Stalker because it only attacks at night, is something completely different. It has attacked houses leaving gashes and claw marks in siding. In one incident it completely destroyed a window air conditioner. They say this destruction was caused in part by its trying to get into a woman's bedroom one night to attack her. It appears as an almost demonic like, invisible force, bent on evil intentions. Whatever is going on in this case, to its victims…the Night Stalker is very real.

Giant Human Skeletons

Have they really found gigantic human skeletons? Could they be related to the fabled Nephilim? What's the real deal?

There are rumors and some evidence that certain scientific organizations have engaged in a cover-up and destruction of the many giant human skeletons supposedly found in the U.S. Why would they do this?

The answer is simple. A finding such this would turn the scientific world upside down and threaten a lot of science funds, grants, and reputations. When it comes to rocking the boat of scientific dogma, the scientific powers that be take a very dim view of that to say the least. In short, a lot is at stake for them to remain on the mountain top of higher academics and knowledge.

As for the Nephilim, we will touch upon them later on in this book. There are even tales of a lost city that was once discovered and lost again in the Grand Canyon. It was said to have been filled with many treasures and that there were also huge thrones upon which rested the giant skeletons of humanoid figures still adorned in robes and crowns of gold. The Holy Bible, as well as many other ancient texts, speaks of giants. Even the memories of these beings are kept alive in our folk stories and fairy tales. Remember Jack and The Beanstalk?

So, were there once Giants who ruled this earth? Some evidence does point that way. We will discuss later a very real tie in to all this, the Nephilim, but for now a new chapter in the story of mankind may soon be written and it may be waiting to be found by us just beneath our feet. The real seekers of the truth continue to search.

Hollow Earth, Hyboria, and the South Pole Paradise

Another subject which there have been many books and movies created about is that of a hidden place and people deep within the Earth. This place is called the Hollow Earth. There have been many proponents of the Hollow Earth theory, the supposed existence of a world inside our world. This is actually a fascinating study to look into. A lot of people claim that the aliens and UFOs actually originate from the inner earth and not outer space. They say that this so called mythical land, known to some as Hyboria, is found beyond the inside of a vast cave entrance at the North Pole. Some also say that when Atlantis sank this is where her inhabitants eventually settled. This is another one of those deep studies that could possibly take a lifetime of scholarly interest.

Let us now turn our attention south, the South Pole that is. There are reports that Admiral Byrd actually saw and flew over a tropical type land at the heart of the South Pole. They say also he may have spotted living dinosaurs there as well. Check out his very strange observations that he recorded in his journal at the time. If this is his real account, Byrd has left us indeed with some very intriguing mysteries. Also, it is said that many Nazi ships, planes, and people disappeared at the end of World War II as the Third Reich crumbled. It is said too, that Hitler fled with them to a secret Nazi base concealed in this tropical land at the South Pole. It is told that the base is still there and that the flying saucers people see actually originate from that base.

There are some reports of a possible worldwide network of tunnels connected to the Earth within the Earth. That research is waiting on an internet search engine near you. This theory will result in very strange research for sure. One more note on this extremely high strangeness, I find it interesting, as a scholar of folklore, that there are many tales and legends of people and races that are supposedly found underground.

So what is really beneath us? One of the scariest places on Earth is supposedly the catacombs of Paris. I find it interesting that those who visit Paris, most of the time, never realize what a strange and frightening place lies just below their feet. Whenever I hear stories of the Hollow Earth an ancient maxim always comes to mind: As Above, So Below. Of course, this is speaking of Heaven and Earth, but it does make one wonder what could be really going on below. It makes you wonder too that if this could be one possible explanation for the mysterious worldwide humming sound heard by so many people. It truly is a strange planet we live on.

Reptilian Aliens

Over the years there have been many reports of strange encounters with what can only be described as humanoid, alien like reptilian creatures. People that have studied these creatures also call them Reptoids. The sightings are most prevalent among cavers (spelunkers who explore cave systems).

There is a story of a teenage boy who was investigating a mysterious tunnel that was situated in one of the mid-western states in the United States. Thinking it was somehow connected to a secret Government complex, he was observing the mouth of the cave when, to his astonishment, he saw two large Reptilian beings (large being that they were around six to seven foot tall he estimated) walk out of the entrance, look around for moment, then go back inside. He said that he had the feeling that they knew he was there. The Reptoids were wearing jumpsuits and what he did see of their skin, was a dark shade of green. It was a color shade very much, like he said, to that of an iguana.

Spooked by what he'd just witnessed, he was leaving the area as fast as possible through the surrounding woods, when he was accosted by two armed soldiers in black. These soldiers roughly escorted him out of the wooded area with the threat of jail if he ever returned. Some say the boy was very lucky. It could have gone a lot worse for him. Sightings of these creatures are often in supposed proximity to secret military bases.

Some have even been seen in cooperation with their human military counterparts on military operations. So what is really going on here? Are the imaginations of some people really working overtime? Are these beings really aliens from out there or, as some have come to speculate, or are they perhaps Earthly in origin, existing secretly alongside mankind for centuries? Still others bring into play the Demonic card. Have not many so called descriptions of demons been related to their reptilian look? Remember the biblical description of Satan, that old serpent, the dragon, the devil. What is really going on with these so called reptilians? Is it simply just rumor? Or, is there a deeper mystery here that may threaten our very world? We urge you to look further into these many strange and disturbing reports. Are there really monsters like this beneath us, in the darkest of places? You decide!

The Mysterious Black Vehicles

Both authors of this book have each had experiences with these strange SUVs. We will speak more on that later. We have heard of others who have also encountered, The Mysterious Black Vehicles. They are, seen often in convoys on interstate highways, sometimes, escorting unmarked semi trucks. They are often seen in and near military bases and, as some paranormal researchers and investigators will tell you, they are sometimes shadowed by these black, unmarked, and dark window tinted vehicles.

These SUVs are definitely known to be government related, their government tags often give them away fairly easily. Sometimes they are seen in close proximity to areas of drone activity. Also, they are reported in places where any paranormal activity, at least the kind we know as high strangeness, has taken place or has been reported. It is said that if you try to approach or acknowledge one of these SUVs, they will drive away immediately.

They are, it seems, interested in a wide range of subjects. They are seen at sightings about everything from Bigfoot, portal reports, alien big cats, to UFOs. It would seem they have a vast interest in everything considered strange and paranormal. The owners of these mystery vehicles have been known to harass witnesses of the paranormal and attempt to keep those same people under observation.

What do they want? What are they really up to and why are they watching? What part of our government do they work for and what are their true motives? Are they even a part of the government at all? There are many questions about The Mysterious Black Vehicles and even fewer answers. They are real and they are watching. It is sad to note, that your government is no longer your friend in any way. Let us hope it doesn't become your worst nightmare.

Brandon's Encounter with the Mysterious Black Vehicle

I have never put too much thought into the mysterious black government SUVs until Dennis and I had a conversation about them one day. He was telling me his story of how he had been followed by a mysterious black SUV and, of course, I became a little paranoid about it. A few months went by and I began to let my guard down. I figured that the government would never be interested in me. That seemed to change when our group decided to go to the media about our findings on Bigfoot. First, I got a call from a few members asking about these "stupid little flying things" buzzing around our research area. The first thing that came to my mind was a drone, so I asked what they looked like and what our members described was a drone. I then began to get that uneasy feeling again. I started to watch for drones and black SUVs and this time I was not disappointed.

I live nowhere near our research area and I began to see drones flying around my house. It was not very often, but I did see them. I do not think that the drones continued to fly very much over my house after our initial observation, but they do continue to fly over our research area to this day.

After the drones stopped I began to notice the same black SUV everywhere I went. At first I thought that I was only being paranoid because of the flying drones and then I began to take closer looks. I was never in a good enough position to the see the tag but I could tell from how the vehicle was made that it was the same one.

At first I was worried, but then I thought to myself that they were only observing. I was strangely okay with that. I began to get curious about the SUV. When I was at home they would park at a house that had been vacant for some time. The owners had passed away and their children were coming in and out, but they would not stay very long. My curiosity finally got the better of me.

One evening I left work and saw this same SUV get behind me on the interstate. I have no idea where they were parked, but they were definitely behind me. When I noticed this I decided to take a strange way home. If it were me just being paranoid they would not have followed me. Well, as luck would have it, they followed me every mile.

I usually get the mail before parking my vehicle, but I thought this time I would park then go to the mailbox. I wanted to see if that SUV was in the driveway of the vacant house. Sure enough it was. I finally had enough, so I decided to do something about it. I just smiled and waved.

I really did not expect any reaction, however, as soon as I waived the SUV backed out of the driveway and began to drive toward me. As it rolled toward me I wanted to see who was in there, but all of the windows were tinted, including the windshield. Even the tag had some sort of cover over it. After the SUV drove past me, it sped up and I have yet to see it again.

It could have been simply a fluke, but I do not know many vehicles that look exactly the same. I am not sure if I was being watched or not, but one thing is for sure, I am definitely checking behind my shoulder more often now.

Dennis' Encounter with the Mysterious Black Vehicle

I, like Brandon, has also had a recent encounter with the black unmarked government SUVs, once again.

While in the process of co-writing this book that you're reading, I was arriving home in the late evening and about to unlock my door when I noticed a black SUV going slowly by my house. Now my home is situated around thirty feet from the street in front, so I was not very far away from this vehicle. What really caught my attention was its behavior, as it was driving rather slowly down the street, especially when it got in front of my house. As soon as it passed by, it sped up, as it went further on down the street.

Since I'd gone through this kind of thing before, the incident I related earlier in this book about when I first brushed shoulders with high strangeness, I was instantly suspicious. I immediately stepped back into the shadows of my porch and waited. Sure enough, in a few minutes it came back around the block and again drove slowly going by my house. As soon as it passed this time, I walked out on my walkway and watched it further on down the road. The black SUV turned onto a side road down the street from my house and stopped. It sat there for a few minutes and then drove off out of sight. I walked back to the porch and waited a few minutes and then I decided to walk out to the sidewalk in front of my house and stand by my mailbox. It was only a minute and here it came again. Only this time, it could I'm sure, see me clearly in its headlights. This time it picked up speed and quickly passed me. It then was gone down the road and off into the night. This last time, however, I caught a quick glimpse of the U.S. Government tag at its rear. It was hard to tell, as the tag had some kind of covering over it.

"Hmm," I thought. It seems some parties are still interested in me. It only proved to me that strange days are still ahead.

Another really odd incident I'd like to relate here, that took place a couple of weeks before this, is what happened at the time we lifted the eighteen inch footprint casts from the research area. That evening, I brought the casts home with me, for Brandon and I to get together and clean them in the next few days. That night, something really strange took place. My dog Zach, who I mentioned in the UFO incident earlier in the book, woke me up around one A.M. Keep in mind that I do know his different barks well. The way he was barking was an indication that there was something or someone outside. I immediately dressed and grabbed my handheld spotlight. I opened the door and let him out first and then I followed. He went storming around the house barking ferociously.

He was definitely acting as if someone had just left the yard. My house is surrounded by a chain link fence with several gates, one of which leads out to the patio and backyard.

I always keep it closed to keep Zach from going on night hunting expeditions alone, but the gate was wide open. This was very strange indeed. I live there alone and I know that the gate should have been closed. I also had the feeling that this incident was not a stray cat, but more like a human presence that had recently been there. Then it hit me, I remembered the casts still in the back bed of the truck. Nervously I checked the back and gave a sigh of relief when I found they were still there. Of course I immediately took them back in the house with me. The many years I've lived there, I've never had an incident of this kind take place and I am a very observant person.

It was a very strange incident, that I really can't judge honestly one way or the other for lack of evidence. However, it was really a weird coincidence, especially on the very night I brought those casts home that this took place. Was someone really prowling around my yard and were they looking for those casts? I do not know for sure, but I do know this, the longer I deal with things of the paranormal and high strangeness the more I come to realize, that there just may not be anything such as coincidence.

The Philadelphia Experiment

This is definitely another paranormal subject that many books have been written and a few movies have been made as well. It is one of the strangest of stories in science and science fiction. It has reached legendary status over the years. The story goes that a strange experiment was conducted on a battleship during World War II.

The experiment was to make a ship invisible to radar. It supposedly worked all too well as it actually not only turned the ship completely and physically invisible, but teleported it through space and time, to another port many miles away and back again. Einstein himself was said to have witnessed some of this effect, as it was all based on his unified field theory. However, they say that some of the men on the ship died under very mysterious circumstances. It is told that some sailors re-materialized part of the way into metal bulkheads, while others suffered partial periods of invisibility and madness.

What really happened that strange day in that naval yard? What is legend or what is fact? Many years ago, Vincent Gaddis wrote a very interesting book on this and other high strangeness subjects, titled *Invisible Horizons*. He theorized that those in the government at the time were so scared by what took place with the Philadelphia Experiment, that they tabled it, covered it up, and put it under wraps until such time as they thought that the technology could be safely and intelligently used for their purposes. It is told to this day, that all this strange tech is at the basis of modern day stealth technology and behind many of the Army's experiential excursions into invisibility that were said to be on trial in Afghanistan and Iraq. So, you might say that the Philadelphia Experiment continues to this day.

What do you think? Is it legend and myth, or is it reality? No matter what you think about these things don't forget one thing…all legends have some basis in fact.

Rogue Scientists and the Z-virus

It has been rumored for a while now that there are men and women of science, mad scientists to be more precise, who are working in secret labs of their own design. They are working on a doomsday formula known as the "Z" Virus. The "Z" of course stands for Zombie. They are supposedly working to bring about a Zombie Apocalypse into the world and destroy civilization and mankind as we know it.

These self made Frankensteins, are said to be working diligently on their own brand of chemical warfare. Some are said to even be subsidized by certain elements in the government or devious corporations.

We want to pause here for a moment and ensure that something is clear to the readers. Real zombies, yes there are real zombies, are mindless souls who have been robbed of their willpower and made into slave labor. They are very prevalent in the Caribbean, where voodoo reigns supreme. They do not eat people, ghouls, not zombies, eat people.

The ghouls of horror and folklore and human ghouls, such as some serial killers, are the real eaters of human flesh. The misconception of brain eating zombies is purely an invention and an error of Hollywood. If we are made into mindless killers by some strange mutated mad cow disease that should infect us, or if we are truly the walking dead due to this or some other condition, why would we need to eat? Dead and reanimated corpses do not need sustenance to continue as living organisms, as they are no longer alive.

That is enough of that, back to the crazy scientists in their home made labs. Why would anyone want to destroy everything as we know it, in such a horrible way? The stories also give a motive, a financial one. To hold the world hostage, would be to pull off the greatest extortion gambit ever known. The ransom of civilization could be untold billions of dollars in gold. So, is this just a crazy story? Could this really happen and are their people working right now toward this end? Let's hope this is just a rumor. However, ask yourself, what if even a little of this story is true? All it would take is for one person to get the formula of the "Z" virus just right, for all of the wrong reasons.

Shadow People

Who or what are the Shadow People? They are said to be shadow shaped beings or entities that can appear almost anywhere. Some have been described as wearing hats, robes, as well as other types of clothing. They are often seen in so called haunted locations and they have been known to harass people for years. They have in some cases been reported in alien abductions and are seen often in correlation with Demonic activity.

Demonologists think that these shadow beings are just another form that demons take in which to manifest themselves. These entities have been said to physically attack and torture their victims. This is the exact modus operandi of the demonic. It is a known fact that shadow people have been driven out of places and lives, by religious means.

There is another theory that the shadow being is a creature of some other strange dimension, which is just passing through our reality. However, when you look at the interaction that they take in regards to those they meet, this theory seems somewhat lacking. The shadow people seem many times to look upon people as enemies or someone to torture and hurt. There has been no known enemy to mankind that acted in this way, but the demonic.

If you have seen these things on a regular basis or have been or are being visited by the shadow people, we urge you to get help immediately! With the shadow people, things can often go from bad to worse, very quickly.

The Nephilim

This is a very interesting subject. The Nephilim are thought to be the offspring of fallen angels and humans. They are said to be half demonic and very evil. In ancient times they were thought to be the fathers of giants as well. It is often said too, that they are demons in human form who can and do interact and function as individuals and invaders of a sort in the world of man. They have been rumored to be in places of high positions throughout our society and are quietly laying the ground work, for a complete takeover of this world by the forces of darkness. Should you by accident ever discover their true identity, they will hunt you down and kill you or you will simply and mysteriously disappear.

On a side note, it is also thought by some Demonologists that during a sexual attack by a succubus on a man, the demon can take some of the man's semen and then in incubus form impregnate a female human. The offspring of this unholy union would also be considered a type of Nephilim.

Do the fabled Nephilim really exist? When it comes to the demonic realm, anything is and can be possible.

Pazuzu / Zozo

Having done well over a thousand cases in and related to the paranormal field and many of them being consultation cases dealing with the demonic, we can say without a doubt, that Ouija boards are bad news. We have seen far too many cases related to their use, to ever in anyway consider them a simple harmless toy. There are indeed many recorded instances where the use, or shall we say misuse, of this instrument has opened dark spiritual doorways that were best left alone. If you are still of the opinion that Ouija boards are a harmless toy, we want you to think of it this way. It is not the object itself that is harmful; it is the intent behind its use. Water is a necessity, but if you hold someone's head under water they will suffocate. Therefore you have taken something that is seemingly harmless and, with intent, used it for nefarious purposes.

That being said, we are now turning our attention to the reports of many researchers who have all had the same strange experience of the same entity communicating with them through the spirit board. This entity likes to call itself Zozo in most accounts. Let us explore who or what this may really be.

There are some Demonologists who claim that the name Zozo is a cryptic way of saying the name Pazuzu. In Assyrian and Babylonian mythology, Pazuzu (sometimes Fazuzu or Pazuza) was the king of the demons of the wind, and son of the god Hanbi. Pazuzu represented the southwestern wind, the bearer of storms and drought. He also supposedly has another name, his Christianized name, which is Beelzebub, a chief demon and Prince of Hell. He is a very bad demon to tangle with. His powers are said to be second only to Satan and some claim he is even Satan himself.

As we said at the beginning of this section, this name, Zozo, keeps occurring time after time in Ouija board communication. This name continually comes up in different parts of the world where people who have no connection to each other at all. This name also comes up in different centuries as well.

The modern version of the talking board, as we know it today, was invented in the late eighteenth century. This name not only showed up then, but again in the nineteenth and twentieth centuries as well. What's going on here? Is someone giving us some clues or playing some kind of weird game with us? Could that someone be Pazuzu? Could it be some genetic disposition that makes all involved involuntarily spell out the name? Or is this some kind of diabolical demonic influence?

There are many people that claim this to be true. Demons are said to be very egotistical beings that love their own notoriety. The ancient texts that tell of the Demon Lord Pazuzu, also state that when this very powerful demon gets a hold on someone he never lets go and he haunts those that are his victims, until they die. It may be a good idea to remember that the next time someone pulls out an Ouija board. After all it's just a game, right?

Thunderbirds

One of our favorite cryptids is the fabled Thunderbird. To the Native American Indians he resembled a great dark hawk or eagle like bird. When the Thunderbird rode upon the winds of a great storm, the sound he made with his wings was the mighty voice of the thunder. That is how the Thunderbird received its name. In modern times however, some descriptions of this creature have him resembling something from the age of the dinosaurs. Some, who claim sightings, say he looks more like a huge pterodactyl or pterosaur. The beast is said to fly with gigantic leather like bat type wings and has a lizard head with a beak. The thunderbird, whether it is with feathered wings or leather, is an enduring North American legend. It has a counterpart that is found in the Middle East called Roc. Of course there is also the mystical and mythic Phoenix of old.

The only known bird of a size that might come close to the thunderbird is the North and South American Condor and the legendary huge bird called Washington's Eagle. However, they pale in comparison to the reported wingspan of the thunderbird, which is said to be as large as that of a small airplane. Does the thunderbird really exist? A lot of people are reporting supposed sightings of these big birds or flying cryptids. If you should ever spot one, be sure to let us know. We would love to see something as magnificent as this creature would be.

Elementals and the Djinn

This is the strange spiritual side of high strangeness. Let us first look at the Djinn. Some scholars say that the Djinn are the Islamic equivalent of the Judeo-Christian Demons. However, it should be noted, that there is a lot of dark magic associated with the Djinn, whereas the demonic has more of an undefined paranormal or supernatural element to it. The Djinn are thought by many in the Middle East, to be at times, good and bad, but mostly bad. They are especially bad to those who do not respect them.

Like the case of the skin walkers we looked at earlier, most people who believe in the existence of the Djinn, are afraid to talk about or acknowledge the subject. They are wary of drawing the attention of the Djinn. In their origin, the Djinn were created by God, out of smokeless fire and hence they are widely associated with this element. They were thrown out of Heaven because that would not bow to God's greatest creation…humans. They are said to haunt caves and desolate places and are said also to have an evil influence over not only people, but animals and objects as well. They are also said to guard great treasures of which they are very possessive.

It is also told, that like Demons, the Djinn can be captured or tricked into containers. That of course is where the genie in a bottle legend comes from. One should always be careful of what is opened and what you might wish for.

Now let us turn to the elementals. The number and influence on culture of these beings is very large. They range from the elves, gnomes, brownies, ogres, fairies (faeries in Ireland), pookas, mermaids, banshees, demons, kelpies and the list goes on and on.

They are thought, by scholars of the Demonic, to be a class of Demons that use known images to deceive their victims. Others say that the elementals are demons that were once heavenly spirit creatures that were thrown to earth and they are now tied forever to the known elements of the universe and the earth itself. This gives way to their name, elemental spirits.

Let us take for instance the faeries. They are far from the Disney Tinker-bell image that you know. They are full human sized figures who are dark beings of power. In Celtic tradition they are tied directly to the The Tuath(a) Dé Danann. This phrase is usually translated as "people of the goddess Danu." They are also known by the earlier name Tuath Dé or "tribe of the gods." Faeries are said to be a race of supernaturally-gifted people in Irish mythology. They are thought to represent some the main deities of pre-Christian Ireland. Yes, these beings are far from Peter Pan alright. The excellent paranormal writer and legend seeker, Barry Fitzgerald has several good books on the subject of Irish Faeries and Elementals along with other strange creatures. One of our favorites is *In the Mist of Gods*. His books make for some very interesting reading on this subject.

Like the Faeries, the Tuath(a) Dé Danann were also said to a very secretive race of people who kept mostly to themselves and lived underground. Most of the High Clans or Septs of Ireland are supposed to be descended from this tribe. There are many places in Scotland and especially Ireland that are said to be haunted by elemental spirits, who wield a dark and dreadful ancient power. The people of that beautiful green island will quickly tell you, that it is best to leave alone, what cannot be understood.

Phantom Black Cats

Another truly strange cryptid is Phantom Black Cats. These cryptids
are spotted in many places throughout the world. What we are
talking about here is not the house cat variety of black cats, but a
very large and very black, leopard like, jungle feline. These cats
seem to mysteriously appear and disappear, hence the designation,
Phantom Black Cats. It should also be noted here that there are
other colors of this animal reported as well, but the largest number
are those of the coal black variety.

As paranormal investigators, we hear about these sightings from
time to time. We have looked into a few cases and talked to many
hunters who claim sightings of these mysterious creatures.
Sometimes a footprint can even be found, rarely scat, and an
occasional photo can be shown as evidence. However, the best way
to go about finding these creatures is to stake out the location
where one has been spotted. Sometimes, if an animal is familiar
and comfortable in its territory, it will return to the same vicinity.

Most wildlife experts and forest rangers will however, laugh at you
when you bring up this subject, so be prepared. They will tell you
that black cougars do not exist and that black leopards and jaguars
are found only in zoos. However, many people have seen that this is
not true at all. Like a lot of people, the experts, often only believe in
what they can see. It's not that farfetched that some of these
sightings could be zoo animals or privately owned animals that have
escaped or have been released. It should also be said, that this theory
could not explain all of the many reports that are given.

The writer of many excellent paranormal books, Nick Redfern, a personal favorite author and researcher of ours, has speculated that there could also be another factor in the case of Phantom Black Cats, a possible demonic one. In certain instances of dark and arcane witchcraft and satanic rituals, it is told that demons in the form of these large black cats were said to haunt the immediate area where these devil raising spells were performed, even many years after the fact. In his very intriguing book *Monster Diary*, Mr. Redfern notes an historical account of an archaic ritual and incantation called The "Taigheirm." In its horrific execution, it is said to raise Demons in the form of gigantic black cats.

So what do you think? Is someone missing his very large and very dangerous pet? Are these animals really unnatural, demon cats? Have they been here the entire time and we have just not noticed? Have these creatures wandered here via a portal of some kind? If so, where did these (ABC) Alien Big Cats originally come from? Are they simply exotic animals released in the wild or something far stranger? Like all things of the weird and mysterious, the Phantom Black Cats carry with them, far more questions than answers.

Etcetera...Etcetera...Etcetera

We could go on and on with this section, with such things as the many cases of cattle mutilations as well as human mutilations that occur. We could mention the strange story of the NASA rocket scientist Jack Parsons who was a disciple of Alastair Crowley. He retired to his home near Devil's Gate Dam in Southern California to work on strange occult experiments, one of which was called The Babylon Working. This is a ritual to bring The Whore of Babylon, spoken of in the bible, into this world by opening a dark spiritual door. Some speculate that opening that gateway is why he died a horrible death. There are also the strange disappearances of several children near his home that also may figure into his bizarre life and the legacy he may have left behind.

Then we could also look into the strange paranormal happenings that occur regularly along the 37th parallel of North America. What about all the many mysterious disappearances of people in our national parks, why are their fake cell towers, what are the strange lights seen often on the moon, and what about those many Angelic encounters that people report. Did Hitler really escape from Germany, what was the actual fate of Amelia Earhart, will we ever know who Jack the Ripper really was, what about all the lake monsters reported, etcetera, etcetera, and etcetera.

We have just scratched the surface and touched the tip of the proverbial iceberg that truly is high strangeness. We urge you to look into these and other strange cases of weirdness, not as researchers and investigators only, but as the interested parties you should be. All of this and more is happening in the world around you. This is all in the Universe you live in and one day, probably sooner than later, these things may come to affect you on a more personal level. Your "need to know" is getting more and more urgent, day by day, whether you are willing to accept it or not.

We have given you just a few examples of the many aspects found in the paranormal field known as High Strangeness, but as the old saying goes, "you ain't seen nothing yet."

Chapter Four

Stranger Days

I believe in the possibility of the impossible, because I believe in the possibility of possibilities.

Dennis Carroll

In the pursuit of the paranormal truth, knowledge, and integrity are the foundations upon which I stand.

Brandon Hudgens

Just because something is not seen, felt, or heard does not mean it does not exist, nor does it mean that it does. If things exist in their own reality then they know of their own existence, whether we do or not. Whether we choose to believe or not has no bearing at all on that…or does it? Have I confused you yet?

It can be very confusing no doubt. What is reality? Throughout the universe, or universes, what you perceive as normal reality may not necessarily be my point of view from where I am. As Morticia Addams once so aptly put it, "Normal is an illusion, what is normal for the spider, is chaos for the fly." So it would seem sometimes that if you are on the receiving end, things will definitely be different than what's on the other side of those things.

Let us talk about that other side for a moment. If portals or doorways between realities do exist, and whether they are naturally occurring, manipulated, or both, would this not be an excellent way to travel from point A to point B without having to deal with that space in between points? You can then use these doors from one reality to cross over to another. Also you could bring things from the other side, to this reality, for whatever purpose you need. Who knows, what may exist in that other plane, just may be the stuff of nightmares. As they used to put on maps of unknown territories, "beyond this place, there be monsters," so let us now turn our attention to the Monsters that may be closer to home and the Monsters that may wait within.

In this world we, as paranormal researchers, have come to realize that there is much more to it than we can physically see. We know that there exists a world beyond ours and that at times this world pulls the veil and we can glimpse into it. We also realize that there are things in that other world that mean us ill will and harm. More specifically I am talking about Demonic forces. The authors of this book are religious people and they have been in this field far too long not to believe that there is something more. They also believe that there are forces out there that are doing everything in their power to bring down the human race.

Demons, in Christian theology, are those angels that were cast out of Heaven with Lucifer for attempting to take over Heaven. They were cast down into our world for disobeying God. For this, they hate humanity. They realize that God has put humans in a higher spiritual classification than angels. This was another reason for their contempt for humans. Understanding that God has given humans the power of free will, Lucifer and his demons use this to tempt us. At times they even use intimidation. This method, however, takes a very long time to accomplish.

Let us begin by talking about how demons can influence humans. Paranormal researchers have long understood the effects of demons on humans. As pioneers, Ed and Lorraine Warren were kind enough to put them in a classification for us. The Warrens gave us the three signs of a demonic presences and they are; Influence, Oppression, and Possession. Later in this section we want to introduce you to another type of demonic presence that we think you may find interesting.

Demonic Influence is the beginning stage of a demonic presence. Demonic Influence begins very minutely and very slowly. It affects not only people, but locations and even animals. This stage generally begins very innocently. Things may move, you may hear voices, things may seem out of place, etcetera. This activity always begins in your peripheral.

The beginning stages always happen as a test of sorts. Most people fail this test because they tell the presence it is okay that they stay. Or simply by their inactivity in the matter, they give it permission to remain. That is the biggest downfall of demonic activity. We are not telling you that all activity is demonic, but why fall prey to a demon when you don't have to.

After acceptance, the activity begins to pick up. You begin to see shadow figures where no light is shining, you begin to smell sulfur or intense decay, you may hear your name called, strange unaccountable noises, knocks at the door, depression, bad dreams, strange and unusual electrical or technical interference, and this is to only name a few. These things happen to not only gain your attention but to wear you down physically, mentally, emotionally, and spiritually. That is how demonic forces gain a foothold into your life. Once there, they are very difficult, however not impossible, to remove.

That leads me to the next stage of demonic presence and this is called Demonic Oppression. It is an attack upon you by spiritual forces. Here the demon is beginning his transition into your possession. Some of the biggest signs of Demonic Oppression are, unaccountable bruises, scratches, marks on your skin, and bite marks. The scratches tend to come in sets of three. The reason for the three marks is the demon is ridiculing the holy trinity.

During Demonic Oppression your bad dreams will turn into violent dreams, you will begin to neglect your appearance and hygiene, your depression will increase, you will begin to withdraw yourself from society, and the list goes on and on. Demonic Oppression is where the demon tries to isolate you from any help. They want you tired, emotionally drained, mentally fatigued, and feeling spiritually helpless. This begins to open the door to allow the demon to attach itself to you. Once it has a foothold in you, there is a long road ahead to get rid of it. Demons tend to plant very heavy and long spiritual roots in a person, once they are attached to that person.

This leads to the third stage of demonic presence and that is Demonic Possession. This stage is by far the most grueling and difficult stage to deal with. The person has a complete change of character and is subject to unnatural temper and rage. They tend to use language that they never used before. The bruises, scratches, and bite marks will worsen. The scratches will appear in sets of three as well as spell out words or occult symbols. This person will also begin to exhibit strange animal like behavior and the smell of animals will begin to emanate.

Demonic Possession is very difficult to contend with. The Catholic Church seems to have the best protocol to deal with these types of cases, but they are sadly very slow to act. My best suggestion is to heed the warning signs before it ever gets to this point. If you feel that you are walking down this path already, please by all means find someone to help you. You can email either author and they can point you in the right direction.

Now that we have discussed the stages of demonic presence as the Warrens defined, I would like to venture forward and introduce to you a concept that the authors of this book have been looking in to. We began calling it Latent Demonic Possession as a lay expression. However, we have termed it with the more proper name of Under Direct Demonic Influence (UDDI).

Have you ever seen a person in a courtroom after murdering someone or many people for that matter and they say they don't know why they did it? Have you ever seen someone in a public office and wonder how they got there in the first place? Have you ever known someone that has done something so out of character and when asked why they did what they did, they had no clue as to why? There is a real possibility that demonic forces may be at play in these situations.

There is a high probability that someone could be under the direct influence of a demon and never exhibit any of the Demonic Possession traits. We feel that this may be a result of the demon trying to manipulate human affairs, attempting to gain access to a certain type of people, trying to make a multitude of people suffer, or any number of reasons. This is a subject that was broached by the authors during a conversation one evening prior to an investigation.

It would not be farfetched to say that a number of politicians and people of power call upon a higher authority to help them in their position. The question is, what higher authority do they call upon? I would not be surprised to hear that some call upon Lucifer himself for help. I am not saying that any certain person does this, or that any of them do this at all. All we are saying is it would not be surprising to us.

Just to stay away from any type of backlash, let us give an example of this using a person that is not real and we will call this person Alec. Alec began working for Company X as part of the janitorial staff and say within three years he is being hired as the new Company X CEO.

Alec may be a Will Hunting savant for all we know, or he could have had supernatural help. For the sake of this discussion we will go with the latter. Alec was the recipient of supernatural help. He gained influence and stature by means of a direct demonic influence.

He is still outwardly Alec, but on the inside the demonic forces are helping him move into the higher ranks of Company X without him truly realizing it.

Let me lay it out for you. The forces of evil are the most organized group the world has ever seen. If you think about the most organized corporation or government, the forces of evil are many times more organized than that. Think about it. They have had 1000s of years to perfect this system.

Now you are asking yourself why on Earth demonic forces would want to gain access into Company X. Well it is simple, influence. This is how demons gain control and it is the first step toward demonic possession. With the resources of Company X these demonic forces can spread their influence on a broad scale.

Now let's think about how Alec becomes the victim of Latent Possession. I don't think that one day Alec was walking down the street and a demon just jumped on him, no. For something as personal as possession there must be something deeper. There is a possibility that Alec made a deal with the Devil himself, or he was a victim of influence and accepted that influence. This would give the demon direct access by means of oppression then possession.

There are many ways that this could have happened. The thing to remember is this, he is outwardly the same person but on the inside there is a demon pulling almost all of the strings.

We often tell people, look around you at the world that you can see, but know this; it is not the only world that is there. There is another and it is unseen. Maybe there are many other so called realms or dimensions. You cannot see these realities, but they exist nevertheless. We must keep in mind, that it is possible, that many of the seen things in this universe are but temporary and the things of the unseen are eternal. This unseen side of the universe, for want of a better word, is the spiritual side. Science tells us that it, like all things in existence, is composed of energy.

It is also an accepted scientific fact, that no energy ever dies, it simply continues on to exist in some form or another. This is a basis in quantum science and physics. There are then many forms of energy, some inert and others of an intelligent makeup and still others that remain unknown to us. The energy that we know of falls into one of two different groups: positive energy and negative energy. If energy can exist on one plane of reality, could it not do so on another? Energy that is no longer organic material is no longer tied to a physical existence. Could it not then without a doubt, on this other level of existence, bend the known laws of the universe? Or, perhaps should we say, transcend some of those laws. In the unseen realm there may be a line drawn that energy, like all things known in the universe, cannot cross, but a lot of strange things can happen on either side of that line. In this unknown part of the universe we might have to consider that there very well may be a slightly different set of rules.

Some Demonologists think that demons may be basic spiritual energy, although the demonic would be considered "negative" energy. We know that a universal law is that positive and negative energies exist and that they are predisposed to oppose or repel each other. A perfect picture if you will, of Good versus Evil. This may be why it was said long ago, that a house divided cannot stand. These positive and negative energies cannot co-exist for long in the same general area without causing some kind of a problem. That is a bad situation indeed.

As in the universe, but not in love, opposites do not attract. It may be a stalemate physically between these two opposing forces, but spiritually we are told that good, the positive, will triumph over evil, the negative. It should also be remembered that it has been said that where there is light there can be no darkness and where there is darkness there can be no light. So, when it comes to the spiritual as opposed to the physical we cannot hold them both to the same accounting. When you open a window, darkness does not fall in, but light can. Why that happens is simple, light is a substance while darkness is not. Darkness is always the absence of light.

A large percentage of our perception of the universe around us, along these lines, is based on the intangible factor known as faith. This force of belief is so strong, it is said to move mountains. But what the truth of that faith is based on is its true power. It can either be based on the positive of the universe or the negative. One is a source of creation and good, and the other the basis of evil and destruction. It should be noted here that positive energy in the known universe is a factor in creation and the negative a factor in destruction. Again, Good versus Evil.

The main goal of the demonic is to debase, tear down, and destroy. They always use deceit and lies to undermine the positive to accomplish this. Since their main objective is destruction, they will always seek these ends by absolute control of their victims. Like one nation attacking another, they will seek to slowly destroy and weaken the defenses of their prey and then conquer it completely. There are many ways to do this, but there are some that always work better than others and they work well. These principles are the ones they like to use the most. You can batter down some walls from the outside, but others will fall better from within. To slowly invade, quietly, is much better than an all out frontal assault. This then is the insidious way that these dark demoniacal forces can work in our lives and in the world around us.

As we have noted many times in the past, even if the presence is not harmful, the demon card is always on the table and must never be ignored. It is a card that must always be played, especially in paranormal research and investigation, because we know without a doubt that these forces truly do exist. We have seen them face to face and there remains no longer any room for doubt on our part. If we truly open our eyes and set aside all bias and opinion, we can see the demonic influence all around us and its effects. It can however, hide in plain sight and appear many times to be something that it is not.

This then makes this enemy very dangerous to say the least and also very hard to spot. Only those with a mind predisposed to the demonic can truly grasp the extent of this influence, because it is everywhere. It uses modern culture along with the media such as music, television and Hollywood, as an important tool. It is an owner of the economic and political sectors of the world. In every facet of our society it has found a foothold that ranges from education to government, to social opinion and individual makeup, and even to the family unit itself and beyond. It attacks us intellectually, emotionally, physically, and even spirituality. The attacks especially come spiritually. This is the way the demonic always pushes the attack. However, it is sometimes so subtle, so quiet, and all invasive in its approach that it can quickly reach its goal, which of course is invasion and complete takeover. This sometimes comes without the victim even knowing what has happened. We think that between the three known factors of demonic attack, that there very well may be a fourth state, which we call, latent possession, we have also tagged it as (UDDI) Under Direct Demonic Influence, as we have discussed earlier in detail.

As we also stated earlier, the main pattern runs like this; first you have demonic influence, with the next level being demonic oppression, and the third state demonic possession, which is a complete takeover of the victim. Now, we must even consider the possible factor of another level between the state of oppression and possession and that is latent possession, which simply means you are completely under direct demonic influence (UDDI) without knowing it and without many outward signs of possession. This state of being is what we think all too often turns up in the headlines of school shootings and the hideous crimes against nature and humanity that we see taking place almost daily. The condition only worsens and is often perpetrated against the innocent and children, always valued targets of the demonic.

These forces would like for you to believe that their brand of spiritual terrorism does not really exist and that this is all the outcome of human evil, which it really is. However, we cannot overlook the factor of the demonic, which of course even under its extreme influence, it still requires the cooperation of the human heart and mind as in the example we gave you earlier. Without even knowing it many times, the victims of demonic evil, by their very lifestyle, mental state, and willingness can open themselves up and deliver themselves over to these dark and diabolical forces that always seek to perpetuate a spiritual act of crime (latent possession) against their victims. This unfortunately can be anyone of us at anytime.

How then can we protect ourselves against this influence and even try to see the signs of latent possession, especially when those signs are so hard to see? Like everything else in this world, it requires work, perseverance, and knowledge, because, at its root, this is basically a spiritual disease and it must be addressed in a spiritual manner. It must also be seen and looked for through a somewhat spiritual eye. That spiritual filter must be used to see more clearly and to see exactly what you are looking for. Also, as a supreme rule for all research, that it must be dealt with in an impartial and unbiased way as possible with, of course, an open mind. The truth of any matter must always be approached and addressed in this way. If you do not follow this rule at all times you have defeated your true purpose and goal and you have invalidated your research from its beginning. Let us investigate now what may be some of the possible subtle signs of latent possession.

The Demonic, as we stated earlier, can attack you in four main ways: mentally, emotionally, physically, and spiritually. Mentally they will seek to take over your mental capacity by using the other three against you, by using the mental tools of anxiety, self isolation, and self doubt. Then they will try to weaken you physically by turning yourself inward with concern and concentration on your own self state. They often accomplish this with illnesses and disease. Then they will go after you through your emotional state by using negative emotions, confusion, and of course fear. Once this is accomplished they will seek to confound and darken you spiritually by attacking the one thing they fear most, faith. If they can attack you on all four of these levels, then they hope to succeed and end with the complete possession of your body and soul. However, an even more deadly and seemingly insidious attack will be the one that is done in an unobtrusive fashion, so that in many aspects you are completely unaware or are deceived into believing that nothing is wrong.

This attack is so subtle that the trap is never seen, until it is too late. These forces seek to alienate you and cut you off from all family and friends who might offer help of some kind. Then, working on the four states of being, they will hammer you down until they have you tucked away in their box of control. Finally, at any given moment, when your state reaches a certain stage, you are no longer in control and fall under "complete demonic influence." Perhaps already softened up by the aspects of a society under demoniacal influence, you have already been made the perfect victim. The dark forces then can do with you whatsoever they wish, ending always in death and destruction.

You are their spiritual bomb waiting to go off, and just like human terrorists, they don't care who gets hurt. As wild as all this sounds, we are seeing this very tableau being played out all too often in the headlines and news of our world. Sadly too, we must consider in this equation that the victim of this spiritual warfare has all too often opened themselves up to this demonic takeover simply by their lifestyle. As we said before, where there is darkness there can be no room for light. When we allow darkness into our lives, when that spiritual doorway is opened, we then have allowed ourselves to become fair game to the forces that are waiting with baited breath for just such an opportunity. That darkness comes in many forms, whether it is the dark chains of the addictions that can come into our lives, the undue influence of evil people, organizations that may have a foothold in our existence, or perhaps the pursuit of wealth, power, and happiness that has blinded us to the dark things we may do to achieve our goals. Whatever it may be that we have given ourselves over to, we run the ever present risk of possession, especially latent possession.

Whenever we alter our consciousness, whether it is with drugs, alcohol, certain mind and spiritual exercises, or rituals, we open the spiritual doorway to ourselves and to our soul. The dangerous aspect of this all is that we are inviting things in that can completely destroy us, whether by other hands or our own. This is one reason why the demonic likes to attack us sometimes in our dreams.

Sleep alters our consciousness and we are very vulnerable in this state of mind. Are we easy prey for whatever is waiting out there? We don't have to be, not as long as we arm ourselves with three things: truth, courage, and knowledge. These are the precepts of the faith that it will take to fight against these forces: Truth to know what you are really dealing with, courage to stand and fight, and knowledge to use as power over evil. A wise man once said long ago, the only true way to truly defeat evil, is to know how it works. This is a very wise and true maxim.

Courage, on the other hand, can be a nebulous thing at times, but true courage must always stand on the foundation of your convictions. Someone once asked, "What is truth?" The truth in the end must be belief, a belief not only in yourself, your courage, and knowledge, but belief in something and someone greater than yourself. Without true faith in a greater and higher being there is no sense of a greater plan or higher destiny, no satisfying purpose for life and its existence. In short, without true faith you are nothing. As we said before, true faith surpasses all understanding and it casts out all fear. Therefore faith is the enemy of fear. Fear seeks only to beat us down, hold us back, and control us. This is one reason why we are a freedom loving people and freedom from fear is one of the greatest freedoms of all. Faith can seal that freedom inside of us on an individual basis, where it needs to be resolved. Faith in a higher power gives us a foundation upon which to stand. Without faith, how can we ever hope to defeat such a powerful and formidable enemy? This enemy seeks not only our destruction, but to take from us our rightful and true place, in the universe.

Chapter Five

Stranger In A Strange Land

If you do not look up, you cannot see the stars.

Unknown

Hell is empty...the Devils are here.

Willian Shakespeare

It is a well known fact, that there have been reports for some time now, that the U.S. Government has been very quietly contacting certain Demonologists. They have been clandestinely asking questions of a dark and supernatural nature. The question that should really concern us is, why?

Could there be certain people inside our government growing more and more worried at what they may know and are experiencing? Perhaps they are concerned with the information that the government is no longer really in their control? Perhaps they are now becoming more suspicious of the shadows that they may be seeing in the background, the real forces that may be pulling the strings. There have been many rumors in the past and more so in our modern times of a shadow government. Has our country become immersed in a web of lies and deceit? Has almost every facet of our society become the playground of a shadow world? Is the Illuminati, or whatever name they wish to go by, really in control and has it been working in the background for centuries? There are definite clues, signs and indications that this darkness may have even invaded the churches of the world and the foundations of learning and education. Has there been a quiet takeover of the military and industrial complex? It may well be that no place, no institution, no organization, no one, is truly safe from this diabolical influence. Like a dark and insidious virus it has invaded every cell in the makeup of our world. Like most every disease known it will only grow worse with time. Luck may no longer be on our side, as time is really running out. Worldwide media may very well be an important tool in the hands of this force of darkness, a tool for the control of our minds. We can see this now with the news that is being reported to us every day.

These forces are working toward a goal and behind their every action there is a reason and the many clues are there for this assumption. Why are our leaders, public or private, often found to be immersed in corruption and greed? Why are our laws not being truly enforced and sometimes even being ignored completely? Why are our officials seemingly powerless to stop the very obvious breakdown of our civilization? Why are the traditional elements of our personal beliefs and time honored values being constantly attacked? Why is media seeking to control our lives? Why are the censorship and tyrannical overtones of political correctness being allowed to run rampant, seeking a power hold over our existence and even our very thoughts? Why at every turn, are we not being told the truth of what is really, really going on in this world? Why is this evil clawing at the very fabric of our society? One word can sum up all of these questions...destruction.

This darkness is always working in the background, seeking not only just to undermine our existence, but to evidentially destroy us. It will do so unless we begin to fight and guard against its attacks. First on a personal level and then the fight must be carried to all aspects of society in general, then and only then, once we acknowledge the threat, can we ever hope to fight for our existence. The foundation has slowly and carefully been put into place for our complete take over. If, however, we choose to ignore or even believe the enemy is there, the battle will be lost. This battle that faces us is not just for our fundamental freedoms, but for our very souls. Have we reached a point of no return? Looking at our present state we must wonder if we have indeed passed that dark and dreadful place, sometime ago.

When the covers have been pulled back and evil is seen for what it truly is and its influence and intentions are made known, then, without a doubt, you run the risk of that force confronting you and coming after you. When darkness can no longer hide its true intentions, it is definitely threatened in its secret and insidious operational motives. It does not like that at all. In fact, it hates that and it hates anyone who exposes its purposes. You will find a place on its enemies list for sure. They will know your name and they never forget. It is a hazard that all seekers of the truth must deal with and understand. It is a fact that you will come to know as you pull back the curtain of the unknown.

Let us never forget that there are two faces of evil, one that is seen and the one that is unseen. We have touched a little on the unseen. We can now consider a little of the seen although many times like the wind, we cannot see the thing itself, but we can see its effects.

Let us turn our attention for the moment to the subject of the doorways we briefly touched on earlier, those of the spiritual and cosmic kind. It is thought that the diabolical forces of our world often use these gateways for their own nefarious reasons. To get wherever we went today we all passed through doorways and they were different kinds. Some opened for us and some we opened ourselves. Some were already open to us and others we had to unlock. These were all physical doorways of course. We could see them but what of doorways we cannot see, the ones that may be invisible to us. Are they no less as real as physical doorways? Just because you can't see them does not make their existence any less real.

These openings are what we call portals in the paranormal field of research and that is what we are going to talk a little about now. However we must always bear one thing in mind. Once doorways are open, they are open on both sides and it is always a good rule to close a door once it's opened.

It could be that if these doorways do exist, there may be different types brought about by several means. There is the possibility of naturally occurring gateways into time and space as well as other realities and perhaps parallel universes. The science of quantum physics does not rule this out, in fact it supports it. Then we must also look at other portals such as those brought about by the will of the human mind coupled with the practices of black and dark magic and also satanic type rituals. Their basic goal in the dark arts is to open gateways into the demonic realm to power their wishes, hexes, and spells.

Another possible portal that should be mentioned here is that of the alien induced kind, whether that is of the terrestrial or extraterrestrial influence. It is thought by some that these portals exist as gateways for alien travel.

Another portal that should not be overlooked is also the scientific and mechanical means of opening these doorways. A very dangerous endeavor as unpredictable as the rest of the portals mentioned. When one is exposed however to any of these vortexes, anything may happen and whatever is out there theoretically, can and could come through. It is after all an endless universe beyond the possible portal. We must never forget that if these doorways do exist, they could be and probably are as vast as time and space its self and they definitely would be the epitome of the paranormal factor.

There are and have been known areas on planet Earth that are at the origin of some anomalous activity. In times past, these possible areas and certain places of possible portals have been given various names. Such as the gates of hell, the pillars of Heaven, hellholes, doors of doom, entrances to the Underworld, etcetera. A lot of other places too, have known associations with the paranormal such as mountain tops, strange rock formations, caves, places of the dead, crossroads, bridges, natural and manmade, and so on.

Many times these places correlate with known Ley lines, the natural lines of the magnetic field that covers the earth. However, if we connect the dots that the whole paranormal picture gives us and we look closely at the clues, then we can start to see the beginning of possible patterns. As researchers we must look closely and look again a second time. For nothing in this field of study can be taken for granted.

There are also famous, or infamous, places that are thought to be areas of portal activity. The most famous of course is the Bermuda Triangle. There are others we know as well such as the Great Lakes, the China Sea, also known as the Hoodoo Sea, Death Valley, Skinwalker Ranch, the Pacific Triangle, Stonehenge, and the list goes on and on. Let us consider the very nature of these so called portals if they do exist. It is thought that they could occur anytime or anyplace, and therein lays a lot of their dangerous aspects. This could be an explanation of a lot of high strangeness, not to mention strange disappearances as well.

What does one look for when it is thought that they may have or may be encountering a portal or situation associated with a possible portal? Unfortunately, not very much is known about portals. Very little in the way of information or research has been done in this dark area of the paranormal. This truly is a basic part of what we call high strangeness. However, there are a few clues out there if you look and yes the truth is "still" out there.

One of the first and most basic of all instruments in use by paranormal researchers and investigators and one of the oldest, is the compass. It is good to keep one with you at all times in the field. Remember the reports from the Bermuda Triangle and places of anomalous activity, of compasses and instruments going haywire? If you ever see a dramatic change or fluctuation in a compass, then there is definitely something happening to the natural magnetic field of the earth. I would absolutely pay very close attention to this, for it is thought that in close proximity to portals, that there is a significant disruption in the EMF (electro magnetic field). Another indicator of portal like activity is the weird feeling of being out of place or time, a feeling that things just aren't right. During this type of activity you may experience anomalies of time and distortion of sight in reference to space and natural dimensions. Some people have reported an unusual humming or vibrating sound that has no definite source or location. Some have also experienced slight tremors in the earth. There have been sightings of strange anomalous lights. There have even been short incidents of what can only be described as time travel of a sort and of course episodes of lost time and even time gained. Often there has been a mention of strange and unusual smells, of something burning and smells of sulfur and even a mechanical burning smell. Then too, there are cases of people seeing these doorways open and UFOs, Bigfoot, long extinct animals and what can only be described as monsters, coming through these supposed gateways. Alien beings have also been reported, coming through and exiting these vortexes. So, it would seem best if you should ever experience any or a even a few of these tell tale signs of possible portal activity, we would warn you to be on guard and proceed with extreme caution. With portals, like most anything of a paranormal nature, you can and must always expect the unexpected.

While on the topic of UFOs, there has been, for many years, a theory of UFOs being connected to the demonic. There have been some good cases made for this theory. Could a lot of the anomalous activity we've been talking about in these pages, be things that are and have been manipulated for and by the demonic forces in our world? The evidence we have seen, leads us to strongly believe that the demonic knows about and often uses the unseen doorways we have been talking about. Could it be that they use them not only to go from one reality to another, but also as a tool to deceive and manipulate the belief systems of mankind and to foster a general negative or fearful state as well? The demonic is very good at using what is already there to use. The demonic cannot truly create anything. Not in the sense of true creation, this is thought to be in the realm of God the Creator only, for it is said that only God can create something out of nothing.. No, they cannot create. They can only take what already exists and change its appearance for whatever their purpose may be. Yes, there is far more to this world and this universe than what can be seen and things are often not really what they seem to be at all. We must never forget that statement, especially when dealing with the forces of darkness. It has also been the experience of the writers of this book that the demonic can and does appear in whatever form they want. We also know that they can take images from the forefront of the conscious mind and use those images against their victims. They can also many times manipulate images of our own thoughts and creations as well. It is very unsettling in the least to realize, that your most deadly enemy knows you, far better than you know your own self.

We touched slightly on this enemy in the last chapter, but let's look a little closer at this adversary. According to Christian Theology, Lucifer, who we now know as Satan or the Devil, was at one time one of the Chief, if not the highest ranking Angel, in Heaven. In the Bible it is recorded that God said of him, "You are the most beautiful, the most intelligent and most perfect thing I have ever created...but iniquity is found in you." This most perfect thing that God created is your main enemy. However by his fall, Lucifer lost everything, because his pride in himself has doomed him to everlasting punishment and damnation. Satan, who was once called The Morningstar and the Light Bearer, instigated war in heaven to take the throne of God for himself. He still has that goal in mind to this day.

When he fell, he took a third (almost half) of the Angels of Heaven in rebellion with him in his fall. Where did they all fall? Did they all fall to the planet Earth, here with us? Here where he still plans to storm the Gates of Heaven once more and sit as God, upon the throne of his Creator? His army of the fallen Watchers, the original title of the Angels, is in place under his command to help him in his war on God and the one thing God loves the most, mankind.

It is said that the fallen Angels hate and despise us for two very important reasons; Firstly, that we as humans are created higher than the Angels and secondly, we are the beloved children of God. These were the two things that the Fallen Angels cannot aspire to be, as they are created beings and not human beings with free will. They cannot feel or ever know true humanity. This will forever haunt them and this drives their hatred and anger. The Bible clearly states that they are reserved under chains of everlasting darkness. Also, in Genesis 6:4 of the Holy Bible there is an interesting statement, "There were giants in the earth in those days; and also after that, when the sons of God came in unto the daughters of men, and they bare *children* to them, the same *became* mighty men which *were* of old, men of renown."

Does this not in a strange way sound a lot like DNA manipulation in order to try and corrupt the makeup of the Children of God, to corrupt and destroy God's greatest creation, mankind? Do you not see a correlation between this and the tenets of Ufology, alien abductions, and new age belief? Are you beginning to see a little of the wisps of smoke of a deep and secretive, demonic fire? All of this is a game of cover-up for the darkness of a shadow world. On this scale, the deception could be mind boggling, the conspiracy theory to end all conspiracy theories. Earth was invaded long ago by an intelligent and secretive force of Alien beings with the takeover of the world and mankind as their purpose. Angels, fallen Angels, not bug eyed aliens, but the disgraced sons of God. Even if just one piece of this puzzle is true, the prospects are staggering. Has there been a deception carried out, on vast levels that are monumentally epic in proportions? Have these intelligences been with us all along? The clues certainly point in that direction. If they are invaders that have infiltrated all levels of our society, manipulating civilization into the direction they want it to go, then are we not in deep trouble? Their best and dependable asset is what Cotton Mather once said, "The greatest weapon of the Devil, is that no one will believe in him." You can indeed get a lot done if your victim does not believe you even exist.

Let us take one example of this influence and possible clue to this demonic manipulation. Hollywood. It along with television is one, if not the leading, influencer in the world today. They can take anything that once was taboo and make it desirable and popular. They mold and shape modern culture on a subliminal, psychological, and often an outright direction of their own desire. Are not a very large percentage of the movers and shakers of entertainment and media obvious socialist? Yes, a good many definitely are. Socialism has been proven beyond a doubt to have given rise to men like Hitler and Stalin. They stood upon the foundation of Socialism to achieve their dark and evil goals. Socialism, which many believe is another word for Communism, is absolutely an important tool of the darkness in this world. Have we unfortunately forgotten the lessons of history? It would appear so.

This is just one very small example of how the shadow world is deceiving and directing the true world. The deeper we look and the more we scratch the surface of this world of ours, the more we can see, what may very well be, the true face of darkness looking back.

It is the stuff of nightmares and it may soon be a nightmare that is all our own. The hour is indeed growing late. It is time to wake up before our worst dreams become our most dreaded reality.

We have mentioned a lot here about the soul. What is so special about the soul you may ask? It was said once long ago that, "What would it profit for someone to gain the whole world and lose their own soul?" Your soul is the essence of you, the real you, and it is immortal. Someday, you will shed the meat jacket you are wearing, along with its limitations and take your place in an immortal reality. If the forces of darkness can take from you your true destiny and give you a place with them in the dimension of their eternal punishment, then they have accomplished their goal of blending their fate with yours. The uncounted evil spirits do not need anymore company…especially yours.

What about you? Be honest and examine yourself. Are you entertaining thoughts you never thought you would? Are you beginning to accept things in your life you never thought possible? Do things that you once considered wrong seem a little different now? Then it could be very possible that you, like the vast majority of mankind, is slowly but surely coming under the undue influence of the spirit of evil that has infiltrated this world. Be very careful for we all must face our unseen roads.

A Strange Conclusion

It's a Strange Universe Out There

In this book we have briefly pulled aside the veil and given you a quick look behind the paranormal curtain. As we stated at the beginning of this book, everyone, at one time or another, has seen or heard what has been there all along. We are chiefly concerned with what lies just beyond the surface. We have lifted some of the masks worn by these age old stories and seen what may actually be, the true visage of an enemy staring back at us. We are connecting the dots and seeing the patterns of these forces that are older than mankind itself. It is a force from beyond that invaded this planet long ago and established a beachhead here that still stands to this day. This enemy has certainly not grown weaker over the centuries. No, it has grown stronger and ever more dangerous and cunning with the passage of time.

Our enemy runs on revenge and is hell-bent on one thing…our complete and utter destruction. This insidious power is the most organized force known to man, far greater than any government could ever hope to be. They are marshaled and organized better than any ranked and armed military ever devised.

The leader of this insidious organization has a purpose that is completely driven by lies, deceit, and influence. He goes by many names. He has been called the Lord of this World and he is also known as the Prince of the Power of the Air. As we are all aware, the air is all around us. It is everywhere, so then is his power and influence. The goal set forth by this leader is simple on many levels. He gives us all the means by which to destroy ourselves and he blinds us to his influence and to the real truth. The insidious fact is not only are our lives at stake, but our very souls are as well.

This enemy is so great that its influence and power not only affects our governments, but it encompasses almost every facet of our everyday lives. The news headlines are being written everyday about this influence. You will find it in your communities, neighborhoods, schools, and even in your own home. You simply need to put the pieces of the puzzle together and see them for what, they really are.

Ed Warren, one of the founders of modern day paranormal investigation, once said, "If it crawls like a snake, hisses like a snake, looks like a snake. Then it must be a snake." How very true this sentiment actually is, in regards to our lives today. The unfortunate detail about this quote is that this snake can look like your greatest dream come true or appear to be your best friend, when in fact it is really your worst enemy. This is the most dangerous aspect of this organization. Its network of lies and deceit run through our world like the dark roots of a malicious disease. This disease can infect you before you realize the danger is even near.

Keep in mind that this enemy will come out and face you once they realize that you know the truth. For instance, as of the writing of this book, the authors are once again encountering the black government SUVs. It looks as though we are continuing to be watched by very interested parties.

For a very long time, however, the power that this organization

held was simply that no one thought that they existed. They continue to bank on that. We want to challenge you the reader now with one thought. This is not some fairy tale but a very real, very possible, and deadly truth. We implore you to look for yourself with open eyes and an open mind before it is too late. After connecting all the dots and looking at the picture that the clues of what we are seeing tells us. One indeed must wonder that we may very well be approaching the "end of days" that has been so long predicted. It has been a favorite conjecture of many demonologists that when the forces of the demonic go into over drive, that they know, without a doubt, that their time is running out. We can see that very thing happening in the world today. Strange days, perhaps, have only just begun.

Truth is the only thing that separates us from our enemy. Truth and faith are the only weapons that we have to keep this adversary at bay. These two facets will sustain you during the battle for your life and your soul. Know this, once you face the darkness it may come after you. So be ready and always remember that in order to truly defeat this evil you must know first how it works. The contents of this book were meant to be an introduction to your education on this subject, not your only education. So do not let this be the end of your learning and research, but just the beginning. Now, what do you the reader think? Are we just putting forth another conspiracy theory? Are we jumping at the shadows of something that may not really be there? You have to admit that all this is no more far out than a lot of other theories out there. These things we have shown you are indeed the true nature of High Strangeness, but ask yourself this, could this all be real? That would be the scariest part of all… "What if it is." We, the writers of this book have seen far too much to know, that this may all be very real.

We simply suggest that you too should look a little closer at the world around you. As the authors of this book, we are well aware that we may lie in the crosshairs of our enemy. This truth we have offered to you may very well cost us our lives as we know it, but the truth is always far more important than hiding in the shadow of our enemy.

We have pulled back the veil and looked into the face of darkness. We have seen the shadows in that darkness and what stands behind those shadows. We are giving you this foundation of knowledge so that you too, may capture a glimpse beyond the shadows, so that you too can be prepared for what may be waiting, down that dim and dark…road unseen.

Ephesians 6:12-13

12 For we wrestle not against flesh and blood, but against principalities, against powers, against the rulers of the darkness of this world, against spiritual wickedness in high places.

13 Wherefore take unto you the whole armor of God that ye may be able to withstand in the evil day, and having done all, to stand.

The Major Fields of Paranormal Research and Investigation

Ghosts, Demon, and Angelic Spiritual Manifestation Research

High Strangeness

Cryptozoology Ufology and related studies

Strange Humanoid Appearances

Earth Anomalies.

Time and Space Anomalies

Religious and Human Miracles

Anomalies of the Human Mind (Parapsychology)

Synchronicity and Strange Occurrences

Historical and Criminal Mysteries

Strange Disappearances

Paranormal Anthropology

Parazoology, Strange Animal Occurrences and Mysteries

Suggested Reading

In the Mists of Gods – Barry Fitzgerald

Invisible Horizons – Vincent Gaddis

Monster Diary – Nick Redfern

American Monsters – Linda Godfrey

The Mysterious Valley – Chris O'Brien

The Mothman Prophecies – John Keel

The Holy Bible (KJV)

The Authors

Dennis W. Carroll

Has 40+ years in the field of study pertaining to all aspects of the paranormal, with many personal paranormal experiences. He is a Researcher and Investigator of the Occult and all things Supernatural. He also is a scholar of the Bible, Anthropology, Religion, Cryptozoology and Demonology. Dennis is a well-known authority on Folklore, Legends, Superstitions, Cryptozoology, Ufology, Demonology and The Occult. He is the Author of several published books on the subject of the Unknown and is a freelance writer who is currently at work on a series of adventure novels based on supernatural events. He is a speaker and does lectures and presentations on the paranormal, culture, folklore, myths, mysteries, cryptozoology, ufology and legends. He is also an Investigator, Researcher, Writer, Scholar, Demonology Consultant for CSPRI Inc and Assistant Director, Head of Investigations, and a Certified Paranormal Investigator (CPI).

Brandon Hudgens

Brandon Hudgens has had an interest in the paranormal for nearly twenty years. He never knew that there were groups dedicated to explaining the paranormal until about thirteen years ago. That is when he began his exploration into explaining the paranormal world. After actively investigating for about eight years, Brandon finally founded Carolina Society of Paranormal Research and Investigation Inc with the guidance of Dennis Carroll. Since then Brandon has co-authored two books on the paranormal, ghost written a book, given lectures, and helped many people to better understand paranormal investigation. It is Brandon's mission to educate as many people as he can on paranormal investigation in hopes that one day someone can take it even further. He knows that we stand on the precipice of a new science and one day the paranormal will be given the support from the scientific community that it deserves.

The Authors wish to state, that if anyone has any questions on the themes presented here or if they wish to report or relate anything of a paranormal nature then you may contact them at the following addresses:

dennis.carroll@carolinaspri.net

brandon.hudgens@carolinaspri.net

Every myth and legend known to mankind is not without its authentic foundation.

Herbert Spencer

Hunt The Night™

The End